STEPPING
INTO
GREATNESS

Dr. Mark Chironna

CREATION
HOUSE

STEPPING INTO GREATNESS by Dr. Mark Chironna
Published by Creation House
A division of Strang Communications Company
600 Rinehart Road
Lake Mary, Florida 32746
www.creationhouse.com
www.charismalife.com

Unless otherwise noted, all Scripture quotations are from the
New American Standard Bible. Copyright © 1960, 1962, 1963,
1968, 1971, 1972, 1973, 1975, 1977 by the Lockman Foundation.
Used by permission.

Scripture quotations marked KJV are from the
King James Version of the Bible.

Scripture quotations marked THE MESSAGE are from
THE MESSAGE, copyright © 1993, 1994, 1995.
Used by permission of NavPress Publishing Group.

Scripture quotations marked NIV are from the Holy Bible,
New International Version. Copyright © 1973, 1978, 1984,
International Bible Society. Used by permission.

Library of Congress Catalog Card Number: 99-75006
International Standard Book Number: 0-88419-567-8

9 0 1 2 3 4 5 VP 8 7 6 5 4 3 2 1

Printed in the United States of America

I've known no book that has informed and inspired me to *step into the greatness* for which I was born than Dr. Mark Chironna's newest book. My sincere thanks to my friends at Creation House for bringing forth this truly different and revealing book.

—ORAL ROBERTS

DEDICATION

To my two sons, Matthew and Daniel, whose legacy of greatness awaits them.

ACKNOWLEDGMENTS

I would like to thank my wife, Ruth, for putting up with late nights and rewrites. I would also like to thank my mom and dad for allowing me to share our family journey.

I would like to thank the Creation House family and Rick Nash, Peg de Alminana and Connie Gamb for their hard work on this manuscript.

Finally, I would like to thank Steve and Joy Strang for believing enough in this manuscript to make it available to the entire body of Christ, and Paul and Jan Crouch for opening the door for me to take my life's message to the nations.

Contents

In the pursuit of

your life's purpose,

there will strategically occur a

defining moment

in the form of a refining crisis

setting you free

from a confining limitation,

thus empowering

you to

step into greatness!

SECTION ONE

THE CRISIS

THAT BREAKS YOU

Crisis—
the gift
that doesn't
look like
a gift

Invitation to Greatness

> The greatest thing is, at any moment, to be willing to give up who we are in order to become all that we can become.
>
> —MAX DEPREE

A FEW YEARS AGO A GIFT ARRIVED AT THE DOORSTEP OF my life. It didn't look much like a gift at all, and it certainly didn't come wrapped with a bow and fancy ribbons. There was no return address and no card from the sender. I so wanted to return the gift, yet it belonged to me—I couldn't get rid of it.

Like most kids growing up, I couldn't wait until

birthdays and Christmas—opening gifts was my specialty. The bigger the box and the more festive the paper, the more aggressive I was in tearing away at the gift wrapping to get to the content of the gift. I loved opening gifts. The older I grew, the "tamer" I was in public about how I opened my gifts. I became more refined, and I gave the appearance of a calm exterior the more I lived in the world of grown-ups. However, the little kid in me still wanted to tear up the box to get at what was inside.

Well, this gift that just showed up in my life when I least expected it was not one I wanted to open. It was a most painful and difficult gift to welcome. Somewhere deep in my soul I wrestled with a truth I wanted to avoid. Something deep inside my spirit knew that God had sent me this gift. It made me question that verse of Scripture where it said that God is the giver of every good and perfect gift (James 1:17). This gift was, in my opinion, far from good, and it was nowhere near perfect.

Some of you may be asking, "What was the gift?" This gift was a nagging question that would not go away, a question that hounded me days and months on end: "Shouldn't you be farther along the road to your dreams by now?"

In my late twenties and early thirties I often compared myself to high school and college friends who seemed to be so much farther ahead in life than I was. They seemed to be more than I was, to do more than I did and to have more than I felt I would ever have. That nagging sense of feeling that life was at a standstill and I was making little progress was far too painful to have to face. If I really answered the question honestly, what would I have to do? What would it cost me to tell myself the truth?

THE APPLE BUSINESS

All the while that this question hammered away at my soul and disturbed my peace, I was also feverishly trying to keep all my apples intact in my applecart of life. I would stack my apples (all the outcomes I had experienced that were favorable) in my cart every morning. Hopefully I would not only display my wares in the public marketplace, but I would also be able to "sell" them to others who needed what I had in my cart.

The apples in my cart were there to make sure everyone could see all that I was involved with and was endeavoring to accomplish. If I stacked the apples just right, someone really important would stop by my cart and buy an apple from me. I wanted others to see and then taste the apples that were in my cart.

Little did I realize at the time that someone close to me (someone whom I would never suspect) had every intention of preventing me from marketing my apples. Ultimately this individual was an instrument God used not only to upset my applecart, but also to turn it upside down and destroy it in the process.

How could a God of love allow something so unkind to happen? If God really loved me, why did He allow one of my closest confidants to betray, misrepresent and falsely accuse me? Why did God allow this person to sabotage all my efforts and mess with my applecart?

Whenever my applecart had been messed with in the past, I would "grin and bear it." I would simply pick up my apples and return them to their neat and orderly piles, stacking them so that others would see their best side. Bruised apples were not an appealing invitation to sample the wares.

When this crisis of betrayal touched my life, it sent every apple in my cart careening down the road. In addition, the crisis caused my cart to overturn and split in pieces when it hit the ground. Even if I did pick up the apples after they fell and were bruised, I no longer had anything available in which to stack them.

With the destruction of my applecart, God was inviting me to give up the limited life I was living and to step into greatness in God. I didn't realize that then, however. All I knew in that moment was that everything I believed I was working for was being taken away from me. That only seemed to reinforce the fears I wrestled with regarding that nagging question: "Shouldn't you be farther along by now?"

I didn't realize just how much of a gift I was being given, yet I knew I wasn't born to be pushing around an applecart. Mind you, there isn't anything wrong with pushing an applecart and selling apples if that is what you are called to do. However, for me it began to drive home another question that was even more difficult to face: "Whose life are you living anyway?"

Ouch! I was living *my* life—or at least I thought I was. How dare such a question rear its head in the heart of such a performance-oriented perfectionist? My life had to be perfect. Every apple had to be stacked just right and polished to the nines. I had invested a great deal of time polishing my apples and putting them in my cart. What nerve to raise that question: "Whose life are you living anyway?" And by the way, where did the question come from, or more accurately, from whom did it come?

There is a verse in the Book of Jeremiah that states, "I, the LORD, search the heart, and I test the mind" (17:10). I am not sure I like that verse; it seems to reveal a process that can lead to a crisis and a crisis that leads to a process.

It implies that "stuff" is buried and hidden in unknown places deep inside us, beyond the realm of our conscious awareness—sort of like the carrot and potatoes at the bottom of a pot of stew that you cannot see until you stir up the pot.

God seems to be indicating that the "stuff" hiding at the bottom of our hearts has the ability to move us forward, or it can hold us back if we don't deal with it. This is a powerful truth.

The Father's way of propelling us into the destiny He has prepared for us is to use crisis to usher us into a process that leads us to greatness.

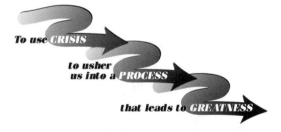

Because of this, He stirs up the contents hidden deep in our spirits, letting them rise to the surface of our conscious minds where we can actually wrestle with them. The Holy Spirit puts what is sitting in darkness at the bottom of our hearts (our assumptions and beliefs) to the test.

The process brings to light those things that have been blinding us and hindering us from stepping into greatness. God allows a certain amount of discomfort to touch our lives so that we will be stirred to move forward and become more fully human than we have been.

Some of the content that gets stirred up and rises to the forefront of our minds can be somewhat disorienting. In the pursuit of our life's purpose, there will strategically occur a defining moment in the form of a refining crisis. In this refining crisis, God sets us free from our confining limitations and empowers us to step into greatness.

The refining crisis that occurs in that defining moment is a combination of unanswered questions that plague our conscious minds (because the Spirit of God is stirring up the contents of our hearts) and the event that jars our attention and demands our consideration in our current reality. The defining moment isn't something you look for—it is something that is looking for you.

Your current reality may or may not be accurately recognized by your heart or your mind. Your perceptions color your interpretation of reality. Someone once said, "Your perceptions are your reality." Without a doubt, what you perceive to be true determines how you respond to whatever is taking place around you. Yet your perceptions can be slanted and jaded—they can misrepresent your reality to you. Without the aid and assistance of the Spirit of Truth, we may perceive something is true that is not true at all.

Telling ourselves the truth is a skill to be developed and honed in the process of stepping into greatness.

Part of telling ourselves the truth requires an accurate perception of our current reality (both internal and external). Here is the challenge: Our current reality is not our total reality.

We are the sum total of everything we have ever thought, felt, said and done. Our total reality, therefore, includes both our current reality and the accumulation of our personal history.

The story of your life is written on your heart. Your memory has stored not only the experiences of your life so far, but it has also imprinted all the feelings and judgments you have made about your experiences. Often when we are not paying attention to what is going on inside of us, we misread in our current reality what is taking place outside of us.

During the defining moment that led to the refining crisis of betrayal, this question nagged inside of me: "Shouldn't you be farther along by now?" When the applecart of what I had been building toppled over in the crisis, I watched as everything I thought I was diligently working for began to fall apart.

God's Wake-Up Call

My "wake-up call" came through the combination of the inner work of being tested by an inaccurate perception of reality and the outer work of the Father exposing a false friendship. When my wake-up call came, my first inclination was to press the "snooze button" on my spiritual alarm clock and sleep through it all.

Little did I realize that through this crisis God was inviting me to enter a process that would bring me into a state of internal balance and harmony. In that state, everything I thought, felt, did and said would be in sync with the core values upon which I was endeavoring to build my life. When things are in harmony on the inside, you can make greater connections with destiny on the outside.

FROM CRISIS TO CONGRUENCE TO COHERENCE

I call this state "internal balance congruence," where my thinking, feeling, doing and saying are all going in the same direction. When we become congruent on the inside, we experience a connection on the outside where we enter into the flow of destiny that God intended for us. That connection between the inner life and the outer experience is what I refer to as coherence.

THE JOURNEY TO GREATNESS LIES BEFORE YOU

My refining crisis was betrayal and the exposure of a false friendship. Yours may be something else. However, the God who takes us all from crisis through process into greatness is in it all, over it all and through it all. I didn't see the crisis as a gift when it arrived to upset the applecart of my status quo. Yet my heavenly Father loved me too much to allow me to remain in a state of limited understanding. Through my gift, He invited me into a broader experience of His greater reality.

He is endeavoring to do the same for you.

What is the "stuff" that is being stirred up inside you, "stuff" that is nagging away at you on the inside?

What are the events of your life that are challenging you to look at the outside?

Does your heart long to connect with your future in God, to discover the flow of your destiny and to make the most of your time?

I've written this book because I want to help you to step into greatness—that is, to find God's highest destiny for your life. Why not take a journey with me through the defining moment of your refining crisis, into the hallway of your confining limitations? From there you will be able to let go of everything that is holding you back from obtaining the outcomes you were intended to experience. It is from this place you will become empowered by the Spirit of God to step into greatness. Will you take the first step?

Do you have the courage to find out what your life really could be?

Destiny

unfolds

as a

dance

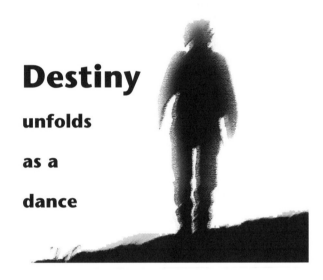

Shall We Dance?

If you are already walking on thin ice,
why not dance?
—GIL ATKINSON

THE HEROISM OF THE CREW OF APOLLO 13 INSPIRED A nation. Their epic struggle to return their crippled spacecraft to earth will never be forgotten by those of us who followed their journey, moment by anxious moment.

While hurtling to the moon at speeds far faster than a speeding bullet, a mysterious explosion convulsed the ship. They didn't know what had happened, but they felt the effects just the same. Oxygen hemorrhaged from the crippled vessel, and fuel cells shut down. A field of debris obscured their view, and the ship gimbaled wildly.

Because the explosion occurred while the ship was between the earth and the moon, they had only one option: to keep going around the moon and slingshot back to earth. But it wouldn't be easy. The computer they had on board wasn't nearly as powerful or sophisticated as many of today's home computers. The gases being vented from the craft constantly pushed them off course. *In fact, they were only on course 3 percent of the time.*

But they were not alone. A small army of experts at the mission control center in Houston, Texas, were working on the problem, down to the very last detail. The importance of their gentle, careful guidance cannot be overstated.

Perhaps the most hazardous moment occurred when it was time for the spacecraft to reenter the earth's atmosphere. The ship had to come in at exactly the right angle—too steep, and it would burn up in the atmosphere; too shallow, and it would bounce off the atmosphere. Theirs was a narrow hallway indeed. In all critical moments, the window to greatness can be missed, and the mission can become a morgue.

Those in the control center had done everything humanly possible to make the reentry a success. Those in deep space were poised in an awkward, yet focused, posture of trust, encased in a small capsule that was positioned between the possible and the impossible, the known and the unknown, the threat of fate and the dance of destiny.

When first reentering the atmosphere, a spacecraft

normally loses radio contact with mission control for about three minutes because the speeding spacecraft has turned into an ionized fireball due to the friction of the atmosphere. Mission control knew that if radio contact with Apollo 13 wasn't regained after four minutes, the crew was never coming home. Those four minutes seemed like an eternity. There was silence on both sides of the divide.

When the explosion occurred on Apollo 13, the crew had only one option—to keep moving forward. They had gone too far to do anything other than go to the moon.

The hallway to destiny is like that—we have come too far to go back to where we started, yet we are not close enough to the future to start living in the greatness God has for us. It is the "PNR," the point of no return. At the midpoint there is only one appropriate choice: *grow or die*. We can't stay still in our journey, or we stagnate. We are either moving forward in the transforming process of "becoming," or we are regressing into a mode of "un-becoming"—where we live a lesser instead of a greater life.

We are continually being invited into the "becoming" process while in the hallway. We must learn to "receive" continually and to welcome the work of the Son, which by the power of the Spirit brings us to the Father. He empowers us who receive Him so that we can move forward in the "becoming" process toward the person He intends for us to be (John 1:12). Once we hit the hallway, it's time to learn how to step into greatness by changing partners and dancing with God.

The Lord of the Dance

The flow of destiny has a rhythm to it, a choreography. It reminds me of ballroom dancing (once you get the hang of it). It has that kind of feel to it.

I remember growing up and watching all the Fred Astaire and Ginger Rogers movies, where they flowed with such elegance and grace on the dance floor. They were so well attuned to each other that Ginger Rogers would follow Fred Astaire's lead intuitively. She felt it, and she moved with the rhythm.

Then the time came when it was her moment to shine. Though he led, he would bring her uniqueness and flair into the overall work of art they were weaving together, and he delighted in her while she did it. She anticipated where he was going, and she could feel it the split second before he did it. I was fascinated and inspired by the creative flow that took place on every dance floor, every stair and even the ceiling in those movies. Wouldn't you like to be in that kind of harmony with God—to dance with Him as it were? I would.

Though the Scriptures are full of stories of men and women dancing, perhaps no account is as poignant as the story of David dancing before the Lord (2 Sam. 6:14). The word for *before* in the Hebrew means "face to face." In other words, this was not a solo performance by David in the presence of the children of Israel as he made his way to the heights of the mountains. This was the visible David dancing face to face with his Invisible Partner, who took the lead and directed the flow of David's steps in the intended direction that He had desired. The steps (dance steps?) of a good man are ordered of the Lord (Ps. 37:23).

David had to travel light if he was going to dance with God. There was a lot he was wearing that would have encumbered the free flow of the dance had he not laid aside the garments of position, performance and external identity and put on the robe of transparency and self-disclosure. Others may perceive us as to our function and our role. But God sees us for who we truly are apart from all of that: transparent, unashamed and following His lead. In the dance to the higher places, our feet become more surefooted in the process. We make the difficult thing look so easy that others observing watch in awe and wonder, breathlessly asking, "How do they do that?"

There is another story in Holy Writ that, if we fail to consider the text in its intended meaning, we might fail to realize there was a Greater David on a mountain one day who was dancing with His Father. Jesus was speaking to the multitudes on a hillside in Galilee. Days earlier, He had commissioned and empowered a company of seventy who were then sent out to bring God's healing presence and power to those in need.

While he was speaking, they returned to tell their story, and it evoked an unusual response from the Master. The Master said that He had seen the Seducer and the Adversary fall from heaven *like lightning* because of the experience of the disciples.

Luke 10:21 (KJV) goes on to say that "in that hour"— in other words, for a portion of those sixty solid minutes—Jesus *rejoiced greatly* before His Father. That word *rejoice* actually implies that He was dancing, leaping and twirling while He was extolling His Father's goodness and love. He had the dance of destiny in His feet, so He flowed with the dance on that hillside while others observed His unashamed transparency before the God of heaven and earth.

Part of dancing with God as He unfolds our destiny is coming to the realization that life doesn't arrive on our doorstep in a neat package. Life can fool us and play tricks on us. Sometimes the very opposite of what we expect to happen takes place, and then we have to figure out a way to turn those moments of reversal into opportunities for seeing the goodness of God in the land of the living.

There is a learning curve in developing new sets of skill. Life is full of surprises, and it takes a great deal of skill to dance with a Partner you cannot see. Much of our spiritual growth takes place in a context of the unexpected. Things that at one time seemed perfectly clear can become completely fuzzy. Things that we thought were pretty solidly held together can become a house of cards. We can lose our bearings and not know how to put one foot in front of the other.

When I was in high school, I wanted to learn how to dance. I grew up in a big, extended Italian family, and somebody was getting married all the time. We saw each other often at weddings. Believe me, there were no small wedding receptions in my extended family. The invitation list was large. There were literally hundreds of people who came to the family weddings, because they were all family. Second, third, fourth and fifth cousins would show up for every wedding in the family (on both sides).

Italians love to sing and dance, and our family was no exception. In a real Italian wedding reception, you had to hire a real Italian band! They had to play all the songs from the Old Country as well as the Top Forty. They had to know all the words, and they had to let my cousin Frankie sing at least one song before the night was over. What can I say?

I grew up on Frank Sinatra, Tony Bennett, Dean Martin, Julius LaRosa, Al Martino, Al Cayola, Tony Mattola and Louis Prima. (Notice how they all end in a vowel? Except those with stage names, of course.) Grandma made spaghetti sauce while the records played in the house. When it came time for a family wedding, everybody had to dance.

Well, I was second generation. I liked Sinatra and the rest and loved the music, but who knew ballroom dancing? I was doing the "Twist" with Chubby Checker and steps with inspired names like the "Monster Mash" and the "Mashed Potato." You didn't need to hold your partner to do the dances we did. It was all about who could shimmy and who could shake—a free-for-all with no real rules or any sense of flow.

My cousins and I heard all the lectures from our parents and relatives on how real dancing was the fox trot, the waltz, the polka, the samba, the tango and the cha-cha. We did remind them, however, that from the old movies we saw on television their generation looked pretty silly doing the "Jitterbug" and the "Charleston" when they were younger.

We felt really awkward when our parents would take us out on the dance floor and try to teach us how to dance the fox trot. It looked great when we would watch

Mom and Dad or my aunts and uncles on the dance floor. I saw them doing a little of what I enjoyed in the movies. However, when Mom tried to teach me the basic steps to the fox trot, I definitely had "two left feet." Arthur Murray would have voted me "least likely to put one foot in front of the other without stepping on somebody's toes."

It took a while for me to get the "feel" of flowing on a dance floor with a partner. I was stiff, nervous, self-conscious, embarrassed and quite awkward. I also tripped quite a bit at first. However, I really wanted to learn how to dance. I wanted to learn it all from the fox trot to the cha-cha, and everything in between. But to learn to dance I had to overcome my sense of self-consciousness. I had to be willing to look foolish, to feel awkward and embarrassed and to press through the learning curve until I was able to dance.

The only way we can truly learn a life principle is to experience it. When it comes to spiritual formation, divine guidance and flowing in our intended destiny, there are no formulas, yet there are *principles*.

We can give mental assent to a principle and yet not experience it. As long as a principle is not experienced in our lives, it is just a theory. Until it becomes a repetitive practice, it isn't ours. And until it is ours, we cannot derive the benefits of its power.

When we begin to discover that there is an end to the hallway, when the light goes on inside of us, we begin to see things more clearly. We see things that others who have been through the hallway can see. They have acquired skills to accomplish that which we have not been able to accomplish. Moses knew God's ways (he had been through the experience). The sons of Israel merely saw God's acts through Moses. They only saw things at a distance and never truly "danced" with the Lord at the level that Moses learned how to dance.

The "feel" of destiny is so different when we finally realize it doesn't happen the way we thought it would or the way some fantasy book told us it would. It is easier to do the "Twist" because we can do whatever we feel like doing. There was no "give and take" on the dance floor in the rock-and-roll era. It was every person for himself. To partner and flow in a dance where two wills become one is an exquisite experience. There is a flow that can't be explained—it has to be experienced. An old Scottish preacher, whose lack of vocabulary was offset by his depth of wisdom, said this in speaking on the topic of destiny: "It's better *felt* than *telt.*" You get the idea.

ADMITTING AND ACCEPTING

The only possible way to learn a truth is to experience that truth. It seems as though the first stage of experiencing a truth is getting acquainted with it. You have to meet your dance partner. If you have never met your dance partner, the truth is that you do not know him, no matter what you think or have heard. Dancing with destiny in God begins by laying aside what you thought you knew "second-hand." His ways are past figuring out.

In the hallway, when I began to evaluate how I had governed my life in the Spirit, I had to admit that it was a hit-or-miss kind of a journey. I didn't know that I didn't know how to dance. It looked so easy when I watched everybody else. Yet when I stepped onto the dance floor, I was out of my element.

Mom was a great teacher. She explained every step that I needed to take over and over again. Although she would normally follow, she took the lead when it came to me. Step together, step-slide, step together, step-slide—she would give me the cues. I would often botch them up and get totally frustrated. She would laugh, and I would get more frustrated and almost give up trying. She made it look easy, but I felt clumsy. I just knew I looked totally silly on the dance floor, and I felt as if everyone were staring at me. I thought to myself, *Gee, if the fox trot is this difficult, I will never learn the waltz or the polka—let alone the Latin steps.*

I had to press through that stage of *admitting* that I didn't know how to dance, and then I had to *accept* that I didn't know how to dance. *It is hard to admit that we don't know what we don't know, especially when we think we know.* Well, I didn't know, and the longer I was on the dance floor, the more the truth came home to me—I needed to admit to myself that I didn't know.

All real learning begins in the place where we admit our ignorance or inability. As long as I hold on to my need to pretend otherwise, I will limit my progress toward the greatness that God has set before me. When I finally admit that I don't know, then I am ready to be taught. In other words, I have moved from not knowing that I don't know to knowing without a doubt that I do not know at all.

DRAWING OUT DESTINY

Education is a process. The word *education* comes from the Latin word *educare*, which means "to draw out." It is a process of drawing out of us what we did not know was there.

There is a place within each of us that none of us can see, for it is seen and understood only by our heavenly Father. I call it the "unknown spot." That unknown spot is the place where all of our undiscovered capability and potential has been lying dormant, awaiting a wake-up call.

A great teacher will draw out of us what is in us—even if we can't see it and don't know it is there. I felt awkward on the dance floor—but at least I was moving. I was doing something I had never done before. At first I made a ton of mistakes. But instead of getting angry with myself (which I did quite often because I took myself so seriously), I had to learn how to laugh at myself. I had never given myself permission to make mistakes. I had to be perfect. *In the hallway, I learned that mistakes are the only way to maturity.* We can spend all of our lives trying to be perfect, or we can spend our lives with the Lord of the dance in the process of being perfected!

The perfecting process involves letting love have a chance to train us. Unconditional love casts out the fear of failure and the lack of perfection if we allow it to do so. Once I got over having to look perfect on the dance floor, I was able to focus on what my mentor (my mom) was leading me into. Step together, step-slide, step together, step-slide—those were her words as she would invite me to rehearse the basics over and over again. Once I had a grasp on the basics, we could move on.

I have learned the secret behind these words of Jesus: "He who is faithful in little things, the same is faithful in great things." (See Matthew 25:21.) *The secret is this: Great things are just a lot of little things working together!* Isn't it true that God is the Master of the great and the small? Isn't that the reason we can trust Him when He promises us that all things are working together for our good and His glory? (See Romans 8:28.) God knows how to put all the little things in our lives back together again in the hallway. And little things put back together become the materials that cause great things to come to pass. Trusting the Lord of the process is so essential to experiencing the outcome of greatness that He has promised.

I rehearsed those little steps over and over again. I did them on the dance floor and at home on the kitchen floor. I did them in the basement. I did them in the living room. I did them in the bedroom. I even did them at times while brushing my teeth in the bathroom. The story is told of the visitor to New York City who was asking for directions from a New Yorker: "How do you get to Carnegie Hall?" The New Yorker gave the obvious answer: "Practice!"

MAKING PROGRESS

Usually there comes a moment when we are put to the test to see if our level of competence has risen. For me, it was the next family wedding. I asked one of my cousins to dance with me. She knew how to dance a little better than I did. She joined me on the dance floor, and lo and behold, there came a moment when the entire family stopped and stared at us—not because we looked silly, but because we looked as if we knew what we were doing.

Once we became aware that everybody was watching us, guess what? We messed up. We had a good chuckle and then kept right on dancing. I arrived at the place where I knew that I knew the basics of the fox trot. I wasn't watching my feet as much or telling myself "step together, step-slide." I was beginning to internalize the skill and assimilate it into my overall appreciation of the art of the fox trot. I eventually didn't have to think about it at all or tell myself what to do. By the time I got to that point, I began to date a professional dancer in high school, and she was ready to teach me the cha-cha. But that's another story!

I had moved through the levels of development in the hallway of the dance from *not knowing that I didn't know* to *knowing that I didn't know*. From there I went on to *tripping awkwardly, rehearsing carefully, practicing diligently and drilling frequently*. Then I arrived at a place where *I knew that I knew*. At that point I began to experience the "joy" of dancing, and that led to the place of new beginnings when I had come the full scale and reached the octave of my experience at that level: *I knew without knowing*.

In the hallway, when we are standing between crisis and greatness, we learn to trust the Lord of the process. We also find that our loving heavenly Father is actively working to draw out of us the potential that lies in our unknown place. It is a treasure that He Himself hid within us from before the moment of conception.

We don't really know what is in us until we allow God to draw it out of us. I am sure that the first time God invited David to dance with Him he didn't expect to do the fox trot with a bear or cha-cha with a lion. However, that is exactly how God taught him how to dance. The Spirit of the Lord used David's "up-close-and-personal" encounters to develop the sets of skill and bravery he needed to occupy the throne.

Once David learned how to dance with the lion and the bear, he unexpectedly found out that no one at the front lines knew how to dance with Goliath. David had already developed a certain set of skills, and he found himself evaluating what the basics were in a dance with Goliath that was similar to dancing with lions and bears. Certain aspects of the principles of the dance were the same, but there were variations on the theme.

David simply took the sets of skill he learned while "playing" in the hallway, and he embraced the opportunity in trust that the resource he needed would be given at the appropriate time. The story of David is our story when we come to pay attention to the rehearsals and practice sessions that the Lord affords us in the hallway.

When it is time to step into greatness, we won't be preoccupied with "step together, step-slide." Having gone through the process in the hallway where we have learned how to dance, we come to rely on the Spirit, who will show us what to say and do in that hour (Matt. 24:36). To "trust the process" that takes place between the crisis and the greatness is to relax in the arms of God. It is learning to lean into His lead in the dance and rest totally in the rhythm of His love and the music of His grace.

 *What are you willing to risk for the dance of destiny?*

My blind

spot—what

I can't see

that you

can see

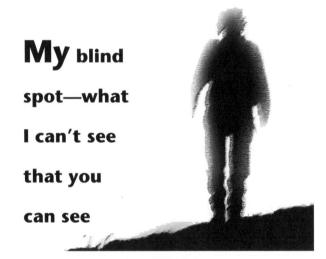

Blind Spots

Some things have to be believed to be seen.

—RALPH HODGSON

I WAS DRIVING ON AN INTERSTATE HIGHWAY HEADING IN A southerly direction at about fifty miles per hour. I had just completed a seminar and was heading back home for some R&R.

The section of the interstate highway I was on was particularly winding and steep, so I slowed down as I negotiated my way around the curves, still maintaining an acceptable pace to get home. A wall of large concrete barriers divided the six lanes between northbound and southbound traffic. Eighteen-wheelers frequently convoyed along this stretch of highway. Occasionally one or two would break ahead of the pack to create a slipstream for the others.

Just in front of my car was a driver in a gorgeous new luxury car. The driver was probably doing well in excess of seventy miles per hour. Wherever the driver was headed, he wanted to get there in a hurry.

I had traveled this interstate highway many times, and I became concerned as he passed me, squeezing ahead of me to find a place in the momentum of the convoy of tractor-trailers. At a moment when I least expected it, he began to switch lanes and enter the passing lane just a hundred yards or so ahead of me.

At the same time, there was an eighteen-wheeler coming up from behind me in the passing lane, moving rather rapidly as we were coming into a really sharp bend in the road. I took a deep breath and prayed—the driver in front was not paying attention, and the trucker to my side was not about to slow down.

The driver pulled into the passing lane without paying attention at almost the precise moment when the truck was practically on top of him. The trucker sounded his horn, and the driver was shocked into the all too common experience of having cut off someone in the passing lane by refusing to check his blind spot. It was an experience he would never forget.

Because two trucks were barreling along together in the center and left lanes, there was now no place for the driver to get back in. So he swerved to the left and careened into the retaining wall. Leaving a shower of sparks in his wake, the driver dragged his car at high speed against that wall for at least half a mile before it slowed down enough to stop.

As the driver hugged the wall, there was just enough room for the trucker to squeeze by both him and the truck in the other lane. God gave me enough presence of mind to slow down in time to avoid a collision. The brand-new luxury car was crushed on the driver's side from front to back. I can only imagine what the driver felt like when he stopped and discovered he was still alive and in one piece.

I had just averted rear-ending them, slowing down just in time—even though it felt as if the event were in slow motion. My breathing was rapid and heavy, and my heart was pounding in my chest. I pulled off the road at the rest stop not far from there and took time just to regain my sense of peace and composure.

WHAT'S LURKING IN YOUR BLIND SPOT?

Somewhere between the rearview mirror and the rear quarter panel of your car there is a space that is quite small, yet it is capable of hiding an eighteen-wheeler from view until it is right on top of you. That space is called the blind spot. It is the place that we were taught in driver's education to pay careful attention to. When we fail to check our blind spots, the results can be deadly. We all have had moments on the road when we failed to check our blind spot, only to invite disastrous consequences.

I discovered something about myself in the refining crisis I endured: I had a blind spot. It shaped my world-view and affected my relationships. It had everything to do with wanting to be a part of things, to be included and to belong. I wanted to be affirmed.

More specifically, I wanted to be affirmed for who I was, not for what I was able to do.

Since that was a major missing piece in my journey, I compensated for the lack of affirmation I needed by becoming performance oriented. I tried harder, worked harder, studied harder and played harder. Yet I found I was just knocking myself out and not getting the outcomes I truly needed and deeply desired. I was blind to my drive for approval and acceptance, so I played the performance game, wearing all the costumes and masks.

Blind Spots Come From Our Past

The blind spot is the one place that we can't see at all. It contains the missing information in the "rearview mirror" of our daily journey that can devastate us as we attempt to move forward and accelerate our momentum and progress. Blind spots and rearview mirrors seem to go together like a hand and glove. The blind spot is the part of me I can't see that others can see quite clearly. It is tied to our personal history and often to unfinished business. It can cause us to be caught off guard when we fail to notice what is coming up from behind us.

Our past provides quite a bit of momentum as it relates to both our present and our future. Depending upon our point of origin, it can affect the way we choose to travel and the speed at which we engage life.

When we are so focused on getting there on time or getting there ahead of time (into the future, I mean), we may fail to pay attention to what is coming up from behind us. Our personal history has some places in it where we formed a way of viewing and interacting with reality that has determined our present position on the highway.

THE CYCLE OF PAIN

Growing up as I did in a family with no brothers or sisters caused me to form a view of reality that was different from the view of reality that my cousins had. Most of my cousins on both sides of the family had brothers or sisters.

I felt left out. I can remember at times begging my parents to please bring home another brother or sister for me, yet my request landed on deaf ears. Dad was busy building the family business, and Mom was doing the books. The phrase "one child is enough" was what I heard often.

Growing up, I dealt with disappointment and even anger at times because I always felt as though I were missing something. I would watch my cousins have times of great companionship as well as great rivalry. I wanted what they had, and it seemed as though there was no way to get it.

It is interesting that at times each one of my cousins would tell me he wished he were an only child, because then he could get whatever he wanted from his parents. The perceptions they had about the benefits of my being an only child were amazing, when from my viewpoint I saw no benefits to it at all—in fact, I saw it as a deficit.

Dad grew up as the oldest son of Italian immigrants in

the early part of the century. He was actually born just about the time when my grandparents landed at Ellis Island and then settled in Little Italy on the Lower East Side of Manhattan.

My grandfather worked hard, laboring with his hands in construction and bricklaying. He later had a coal and ice business on Staten Island. In those days, homes were heated with coal furnaces, and there were no refrigerators to keep food cold—only iceboxes, which needed a steady supply of ice to keep food from spoiling.

My grandfather was a strong and well-proportioned man for his size (he was short in stature). He made up for what he lacked in height in biceps. His arms were the size of large grapefruits and were as hard as rocks. As kids we would often ask him to make a muscle so we could feel the hardness of his biceps. Every so often we experienced that power "up close and personal" when we stepped out of line, and he would give us a swat on the seat of the pants.

Dad told me that at a certain point in time when he was growing up he became concerned at how many children my grandfather expected my grandmother to bear. Dad is the oldest of six sons who lived to adulthood, yet there were others who were miscarried, and one who died tragically at the age of three. Dad never seemed to be able to let go of feeling responsible for his brother's death.

I suppose Dad was about twelve years old when he felt the liberty to raise a question about Grandpa's wanting to have so many kids. Dad asked his father something to this effect: "Aren't you concerned about

Mom and her health? Don't you need to be considerate of her?"

Well, Dad experienced the shock of his life as Grandpa wheeled around and answered him with a slap in the face. He told him never to overstep his bounds again and to mind his own business. Grandpa was a "tough-minded, I'm in charge around here" kind of guy from the Old Country. He was the patriarch of the family. Whatever he said was law. Disobey the law, and you experience the wrath of the patriarch.

I don't want to create an inaccurate impression, however, because there was a very tender side to my grandfather as well. Yet intimacy wasn't one of his strong suits.

At a certain significant moment in our relationship, far into my adulthood, Dad confided that his dad never really affirmed him—that affirmation was something he deeply longed for, even to that day, even after his father's death.

That was a significant moment in our relationship, because that was the most difficult thing for him to give me: genuine affirmation, not based on performance, strictly based on my essence as his son. I wanted my dad's blessing more than I wanted anything else in the world.

It wasn't that Dad did not want to give it. It was more that he didn't know *how* to give it, because his dad never modeled it for him. Grandpa's tough side came through more than his tender side.

Actors want the world to think they are lovers (or at least the silver screen portrays them that way). Yet many of them have learned how to bury their feelings and mask their behaviors behind a tough-guy image. The result: generations of unaffirmed sons and daughters who are driven to perform and succeed in order to get the approval of the head of the family. The cycle just continues and deepens: Each generation produces a new generation that is much more in need of a significant other to affirm them. Those individuals are that much more driven by an unmet need to be loved. Therefore, they cannot be led into the intended greatness for which God created them.

THE CRY FOR INTIMACY

We are either going to be driven by our unmet needs or led by the Spirit—our *Paraclete*, our Comforter (which is the meaning of the Greek word *parakletos*)—who comes alongside us to affirm us with every step we take. We are all crying out for intimacy, yet all too often our blind spots prevent us from feeling safe enough to connect with God's choice of a significant other who is capable of leading us in a way we have not known.

What we have known and been familiar with is "to eat or to be eaten." When unaffirmed, we tend to keep driving as fast as we can to get into the future. In reality, however, we're trying to get away from past hurts and disappointments that keep us driving at high speeds because of our unmet need for acceptance. When we exceed the speed limit, we probably miss a whole lot more of the signals that can save our lives than we realize.

TRYING TO OUTRUN THE PAST

Driving at high speeds because of unmet needs, believing we are racing into our future, we fail to take stock of what is chasing us—and overtaking us—from behind. Tucked out of view in our blind spot, it can run us over before we ever get to our tomorrows. While we long to step into greatness, we find ourselves careening off the road—hurling toward a life of quiet desperation.

These are the questions that are vitally important to ask and answer:

- From what are we running?
- To where are we running?
- How can we get that for which we truly are longing?
- How do we admit we need help?

DEALING WITH OUR BLIND SIDE

It can be painful to sort through certain emotions and feelings. Therefore, we often choose subtle paths of blindness, like avoidance and victimization, for example. Our minds are rather inventive and can create many paths to avoidance, all of which hinder our ability to access our future and our hope in God.

Daydreaming is a way that children often escape from the "real world" where things may be too painful to bear. If we don't grow out of the daydreaming stage, we create unrealistic pictures in our minds of what we want our future to look like when "things will be different." I did that often growing up. I would see myself in another context, another setting where things were more to my liking.

While I believe there is something healthy to acquiring a more positive view of the future, there is also a need for balance so that we don't avoid telling ourselves the truth about our current situations. Ask this question: Do I really want to feel my way through the discomfort, or can I daydream my way into the fantasy of the way I would like it to be? Daydreaming sabotages our ability to access our future, because it is often an escape mechanism that enables us to avoid facing our past.

Since my grades never seemed quite "good enough," I wore a cloak of shame that I rarely took off. I would either blame myself for my outcomes, or I would find a reason to blame others to whom I was being compared. Every so often I would blame the teacher for not being clear in his or her delivery.

I didn't have the ability to know what it was I was really struggling with, so I felt "less than" others who performed "better than" I did. I also had a need to find fault in their performances so that I could bring them down to my size in my thinking.

I had adopted so many unbecoming behaviors that the Holy Spirit refused to let me make any additional progress without taking ownership of my patterns of avoidance and escape. I also kept watching the "reruns" of my frustrations and setbacks in my imagination. In so doing, I became increasingly focused on continued avoidance rather than focused on the things I truly wanted.

Avoidance mechanisms can be quite sophisticated. Our minds never run out of ideas to help us hide. Yet all these behaviors are self-sabotaging behaviors that hinder our ability to move forward and flow with God in the direction of destiny. They provide a way to run from the difficult task of taking responsibility for our inner lives, including our minds, emotions, feelings, intuitions, memories and wills. These behaviors help us to avoid the difficult task of harnessing our imaginations by grounding them in the truth.

These mechanisms provide a means of avoiding intimacy and meaningful relationships. As long as I am avoiding my own unfinished business, I don't have to give any feedback to you as to how I see you or where you stand in relationship to me. I can remain aloof and keep you guessing.

No Choices—Victimization

Years later I discovered that I often felt that I "had no choice" in making my choices. I rarely thought things through early on, especially the consequences of my choices. In many events where there was family or social conflict, my overriding and sabotaging belief was that I didn't have a lot of choices. If we don't have choices, we develop a feeling of being victimized.

Victimization is a sabotaging mind-set, because it places all the blame outside the realm of our ability to change anything. Victimization is a blindness that is utterly debilitating. I believe it is one of the greatest tools the powers of darkness use to keep us from believing the truth and trusting in the power of God to work mightily within us.

KEYS TO INTIMACY

The key to genuine intimacy is self-disclosure. The key to self-disclosure is being transparent and clear in communication. The key to being transparent in communication is being honest about our feelings without venting them on others. The key to being honest about our feelings is describing with words what those feelings are. The key to identifying with words what we are feeling is becoming aware of how we represent reality to ourselves. The key to truly representing reality to ourselves is tied intricately to how in touch we are with the blind spot.

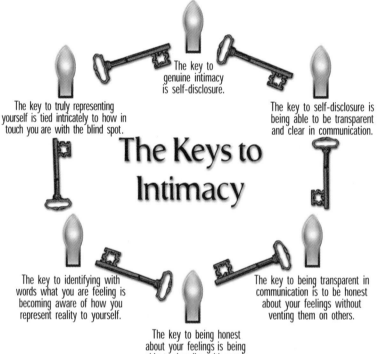

The key to genuine intimacy is self-disclosure.

The key to truly representing yourself is tied intricately to how in touch you are with the blind spot.

The key to self-disclosure is being able to be transparent and clear in communication.

The Keys to Intimacy

The key to identifying with words what you are feeling is becoming aware of how you represent reality to yourself.

The key to being transparent in communication is to be honest about your feelings without venting them on others.

The key to being honest about your feelings is being able to describe with words what those feelings are like.

Over the years of our total life experience we have attached labels to things that define for us the meaning behind an event. Whether it is the loss of a job, a move across country that we weren't anticipating or the end of a relationship we thought would last forever, all of those crises carry with them more than we can fully see at one moment in time.

How we sort through the information coming to us through our five senses regarding those crisis points will determine how we build an altar in our memories to those experiences. The memories we collect are the altars we build in our souls, just as Jacob erected an altar following his most meaningful life experiences.

For one person, the loss of a certain job can be a load off his back, even if he was dismissed for things he failed to live up to. For others, the loss of a job can be an altar called "This Is the Worst Thing That Ever Happened in My Life." Each of us holds our unique vantage point from which we view reality, yet each point in and of itself is not the big picture.

The implication then is simple: We all have blind spots, even when we believe we are in touch with our current reality. In order to see clearly what is in the blind spot, we need some help.

If the gentleman in the luxury car in front of me that day had a way of communicating with me, I could have helped him avert certain disaster. I had a distinct vantage point from which to view what was in his blind spot—I was able to see for him what he could not see for himself.

None of us have "eyes in the back of our heads," although I can remember a few elementary school teachers who knew what was going on behind their heads while they were facing the chalkboard and writing down assignments (now that is scary).

GOD WILL LEAD THE BLIND BY A WAY THEY DO NOT KNOW

As much as we may want to "fix" our blind spot, the truth is that becoming aware of its presence does not necessarily mean we can arrange for its absence. What we need to do, however, is to develop some skills of coping with our blind spot. Skill will keep us, so we aren't caught by surprise when we switch lanes on the interstate highway and find out too late that we can't avoid being run over by what is coming up from behind us.

Speaking on behalf of God, the prophet Isaiah said these words:

> And I will lead the blind by a way they do not know,
> In paths they do not know I will guide them.
> I will make darkness into light before them
> And rugged places into plains.
> These are the things I will do,
> And I will not leave them undone.
>
> —ISAIAH 42:16

Being led into a future we have never known and experiencing the pathway to greatness require that we admit we have a blind spot. The Master said this to those who thought they saw everything:

> If you were blind, you would have no sin; but
> since you say, "We see," your sin remains.
>
> —JOHN 9:41

Denial of the blind spot is tantamount to signing our own death warrants on the interstate highway of our lives. The blind spot is the one area that will get us every time if we don't learn to look back through our rearview mirrors and check out the view from behind us. The prophet Isaiah also made this declaration on behalf of the Lord: "Your ears will hear a word behind you, 'This is the way, walk in it'" (Isa. 30:21). In those matters involving the invisible arena, God wants us to know and trust that He is our "rear guard." Yes, He goes before us. However, He is also our rear guard. We can't keep ourselves from messing up. We need someone to watch with us, if we give Him permission, so that He carries up the rear.

What I know and what I see are not all there is to know and see. There are many things I do not know because I cannot see them from where I am standing, sitting or even facing. I was built to face in only one direction at a time. As I face in one direction, I can focus my attention as well as my intention.

WE CAN'T RECOGNIZE OUR BLIND SPOTS BY OURSELVES

We need to realize we can't step into greatness and fulfill the dream of destiny God has placed within us by ourselves. It is going to take others who care about us, who can help us negotiate our way through those unknown places, that will afford us the opportunity to learn and grow.

The clear promise of the Father is that He will provide leadership and guidance to those who admit their blind spots. He will then invite them to walk in ways they have never walked before.

More often than not we tend to compensate for our blind spots by taking the "easy way" to get somewhere, even if it doesn't bring us to our desired outcomes. Our behaviors become rather routine when we compensate for our blind spots. We often get quite defensive and irritated. We can have knee-jerk reactions to situations that are extreme in relation to what we are experiencing. We can even blatantly refuse to admit we have missed the mark, even when all the evidence confirms that fact. All those reactions are an indication that we are refusing to admit we have a blind spot. They are also an indication that we would prefer to figure things out for ourselves, even if we do get run over a few times by a Mack truck.

FEELING SAFE

The Spirit of the Lord intends to "lead the blind by a way they do not know." For a totally blind individual, the more familiar the surroundings, the more he is at ease in his experience of life. To lead the blind into unfamiliar territory with unknown challenges requires a time of learning where things are placed around them, so that by touching those things they can create a reliable internal map for their safety.

Blind spots have a lot to do with safety issues. Feeling

safe is essential to living a life of wholeness and health. The age-old question—"Whom do you trust?"—comes into play whenever we begin to consider who can help us with our blind spots.

THE BLIND LEADING THE BLIND

We certainly don't need assistance from the person with the "log that is in [his] own eye" that Jesus spoke of in the Sermon on the Mount (Luke 6:42). There are always people who live a life of value judging and who project their own imperfections onto others in the name of God. In their attempts to fix others, they actually hurt them in the process.

Plenty of individuals practice a judgmental lifestyle. They attempt to gain control of others to satisfy their own unmet needs for influence, attention or whatever. This is truly "the blind leading the blind."

When we are unaware of our blind spots, we may inadvertently allow someone equally blind to have influence over us. And because of our own unmet needs, we will keep reliving our past and present unfinished business.

However, someone who has been dealt with by God and who has gone through the initiation process by a refining crisis and has indeed stepped into greatness can see clearly enough to lead us in those unknown paths of which Isaiah spoke.

UNMET NEEDS CREATE BLIND SPOTS

Our blind spots catch up to us when we least expect it,

and we may be run over because of them. Then, run over and lying on the side of the road, we ask ourselves, "Why didn't I see that coming?" If we are overtaken by our blind spots enough, we start asking, "Why am I going through this again?"

What we fail to realize is that our unmet needs create blind spots. Blind spots, in turn, cause us to inaccurately perceive and define our current reality. Since our total reality involves our history, our memory, our present activity (internal and external) and our destiny, it is necessary to learn how to gain a greater peripheral view of life.

How we learned to get our needs met in our past, however appropriate or inappropriate, has conditioned our patterns of behavior now. Unless we are willing to admit we have a blind spot, realizing how serious a condition we face if we fail to take it into account, we forfeit a great deal of destiny and fail to step into greatness.

THE GOD WHO SEES HISTORY WILL GUIDE US TO OUR DESTINY

God sees all and has total insight. When the prophets speak of living creatures "full of eyes round about," as mentioned in Ezekiel 1:18, they are speaking metaphorically of the Divine Power that sees and knows the total picture from the end to the beginning and holds that reality even in the present moment in time. The eternal God is our dwelling place. This God who can see the past, present and future at a glance also sees our particular personal history, current reality and intended destiny simultaneously.

His desire is to grant that the eyes of our hearts be enlightened so that we might know the hope of His calling (Eph. 1:18). The all-seeing God requests permission to lead us by our blindness, if we are willing, into paths that we have never traveled before. There on those unknown paths we are guided into a new future where destiny awaits us. Stepping into greatness involves a process that begins by being willing to check the "rearview mirror" and then placing our hearts and hands in the care of the One who can lead us and guide us into all truth.

The Spirit of Truth comes alongside us as Mentor and Friend. His mission is the total self-disclosure of the Son of God to our souls. There are no blind spots in Him. He is Light, and in Him there is no darkness at all (1 John 1:5). So self-disclosing is He and so intimate is His relationship with His Father that He can say, "He who has seen Me has seen the Father" (John 14:9).

Since there was no incongruence in the man Christ Jesus, His thoughts, feelings, actions and words were all in harmony. He lived in an awareness of connecting with history, current reality and destiny, and He modeled the process and led through the pathway toward intended greatness. He had no need to be anyone other than Himself.

Because He chose to live a transparent life, there was not one place where the Father was not evident both with Him and in Him. His powerful affirmation by His Father as He came up out of the Jordan's muddy waters provided the framework and basis for both the power He operated in frequently and the intimacy He shared with others daily. His greatness was in His genuineness and

His authenticity. He lived a life of balance and harmony within and without. He is our model for greatness.

BECOMING TRULY HUMAN

The Nicene Creed declares of the Lord Jesus that "He became truly human." Jesus showed us how full human existence could be without the limitations of sin. Never did any other man speak, act, feel, talk and live like the Carpenter from Nazareth. There was no unfinished business He had to deal with in His personal life. Perhaps since He walked in the greatness of the Father's love and affirmation, He was able to see clearly enough to help others walk out of the known and into the unknown, to arrive at what they had never known.

Since it is God the Father who surrounds us "behind and before," He can not only provide assistance for what is chasing us from our past, but He can also provide direction and guidance for what awaits us in our future. Either way, God has us covered.

SO GREAT A CLOUD OF WITNESSES

While it might be wonderful to have the cloud of glory behind us and in front of us as the children of Israel did in their march through the wilderness, God will surround us with a "cloud of witnesses" (Heb. 12:1). They have been where we have never been, and they have processed what we are learning to process. These people are sent by God as servants into our lives to lead us out of crisis, through a process, into greatness.

Finding those individuals isn't always as difficult as

we might think. There are many people whom God has hidden somewhere just behind the rearview mirror of our lives. They are watching out for our well-being and have our best interests at heart. In fact, we might not even know they are there and might not even know who they are. They prefer it that way.

Like their Savior, they have no need to promote themselves in our presence or raise their voice in the streets (Matt. 12:19). They are not consumed with an unmet need for attention, influence, control or power. They are content simply to be sons and daughters of a loving and affirming heavenly Father. When they speak, they draw attention to Him.

They aren't perfect by any means. However, they are a bit further down the road of being perfected than we are. They know that real love is patient and sees the foibles and idiosyncrasies of our lives, yet they see beyond our blind spots to what we can become. They long to be able to offer assistance, yet they know that until we are ready to receive them, their purpose is far better served merely to give us their attention at a distance.

They will not force themselves on us. They will not seek to sell us their agenda. They have enough awareness of having gone through the process and having long since stepped into greatness that their chief delight is in communing with the Great One. They have learned from their Master that the greatest keys to relationships are:

- See others for who they can be and not merely who they are.

- Affirm others for what you can see in them that is reflective of their relationship with God.
- Affirm others for who they can become when they are willing to believe that they were created for greatness.
- Allow others to grow at their own pace so that you can relate to them on their terms, not your own.

When we get run over enough by those eighteen-wheelers due to our lack of awareness of our blind spots, a moment will come when we are willing to ask for our missing piece. The assistance we need is not that far away; we just aren't able to see it because of that blind spot. Once we admit to having a blind spot, and we cry out for others who will walk with us on the side where our blind spot has been, then God will send them. An ancient proverb says, "When the student is ready, the teacher appears." The prophet Isaiah said it another way: "Your eyes will behold your Teacher. And your ears will hear a word behind you [coming from the direction of our blind spot], 'This is the way, walk in it'" (Isa. 30:20–21).

What is the most powerful truth that you find yourself resisting?

48

My hidden spot—the part of me I don't want you to see

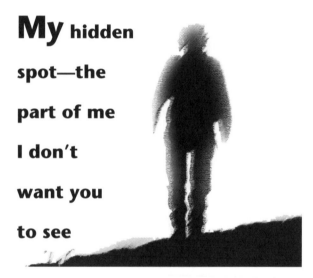

4

The Hidden Spot

A man always has two reasons for what
he does—a good one and the real one.
—ANONYMOUS

HOW CAN WE REALLY LET SOMEONE GET TO KNOW US
when we don't even know ourselves? Consider what
someone once said: "When two people meet there are
actually six present: two the way they see themselves,
two the way they see the others and two the way they
truly are."

We've already talked about the *blind spot*, that part of
me I can't see. Behind the blind spot in your life there is a
place I call the *hidden spot*. The hidden spot is that part
of me that I am aware of, but I don't allow you to see.

There is also a part of each of us that neither you nor I see. God has given it to us, and it is waiting to be affirmed and called forth. It is treasure buried by God Himself, waiting to be uncovered in our lives. However, as much as we may want to jump right in and get acquainted with what is buried deep within the soil of our hearts by the Holy Spirit, we need to first take a look at what we are hiding from others.

THE HIDING GAME

It is one thing to be blind to something in my life. It is quite another to choose to carefully hide something from others. Each of us has played the "hiding game" with areas of our inner life that we may feel uncertain and unsafe about making known.

Adam played the hiding game after he violated the edict of the garden and partook of the forbidden fruit. The moment he ate of the fruit he was more aware of his shame than he was of his disobedience. Shame is a very painful and powerful force that causes us to hide, and it needs to be healed. Yet behind the shame there often are things that we have partaken of that are forbidden.

Our identity is so tied to our intimacy with God that when we fail to stay within the freedom He has provided for us, we cannot enjoy walking with Him in the "cool of the day" (which in Hebrew is actually "Spirit of the day"). We hide ourselves among the trees at the approaching sound of God's presence in the same manner as Adam did.

The sound of God's approach was not new to Adam.

He had heard the sound of God in the Garden before. The Scriptures declare that Adam and his wife heard the *sound of the voice of the Lord* walking in the Garden in the *cool of the day*. Have you ever heard a voice walking?

The actual word for "voice" here is used to describe a thunderous noise. This wasn't a "tiptoe through the tulips" sort of sound. This was the noise of chariot wheels announcing the arrival of a visitation of the Spirit of God at an appointed time.[1]

God had established a rhythm of exchange between His son Adam and Himself. Until that fateful moment when Adam willfully disobeyed and chose to exchange the truth of God for the lie, he had enjoyed the sound of God's approach. As a matter of fact, his chief delight was to know that "Daddy was home."

Every little child that grows up around a dad who loves him can hear the sound of the car pulling up in the driveway announcing at the end of the workday, "Daddy is home." Most sons want to be just like their dad. Adam was God's son. I am sure that if what is in the heart of every little boy today is a result of what was in Adam's genes, then Adam wanted to be just like his Dad.

When the enemy tempted Adam, he approached him based on Adam's deepest longing: to be like his Daddy! Adam wanted to grow up and be like his Father. Even more amazing than that is the incredible truth that the Father has always wanted a family of sons (male and female) who would grow up into all aspects of His nature and carry on the family name.

The enemy played with the deepest desire in the

heart of a son. No matter how you seek to express it, a son has a longing to step into the greatness of his father. Even sons who were abandoned or abused by their fathers carry the longing and desire to have had a father that they could grow up to be like.

What seems so incomprehensible is that according to the Scriptures God had already made the man and woman in His image and likeness. It was already an accomplished fact. By a series of choices they were to transform the innocence of their innate desire into the holiness of their higher calling and, as a result, to step into the greatness for which they were born. The choices we make determine the direction we take. The things we choose determine the results and outcomes that we obtain.

THE LIE OF SHORTCUTS

Adam made more than one choice on that fateful day. Before he chose to eat of the forbidden fruit, which was the external behavior he exhibited, he had already made a previous choice. What the deceiver used to entice Adam was the illusion of being able to take a shortcut and bypass the process in order to step into greatness. The lie that bewitched Adam was "in the day you eat... you shall be as God!" Adam was already made in God's *likeness*, so what was the need to try to be like God?

The lie Adam believed was that there was a quick road to intended destiny. The choice he made was to "speed up" the process by feeding on something that had the power to give him information that God was withholding from him. This choice was enough to cause Adam to mistrust the intentions of his Father. Questions raced through his mind: *What if this serpent is telling the truth? What if I want to be like my Father, yet He has chosen to withhold from me the very thing that will enable me to be just like Him?*

There was something reasonable in the temptation. The serpent invited Adam to ignore the prohibition and accelerate his progress toward maturity. The serpent approached Adam based on twisting the truth. Satan suggested that God was being rather arbitrary in saying that it was certain death to partake of a tree that was actually useful and even desirable. According to the serpent's line of reasoning, the restraint God required of Adam at the forbidden tree placed a roadblock in his way to fulfilling his potential.

That twisted truth was designed to blind Adam to the actual function of that tree, which was to be a place where he judged the serpent and banished him from the Garden. There can be no genuine bearing of the likeness of God without being confirmed in the honor and character of holiness, wholeness, righteousness, well-being and the love of the truth.

For Adam, the choice he made had both immediate and long-range consequences. Those consequences are still present in the world today. The sins of some live longer after they themselves have returned to dust. Since that time there has been a jaded place in the heart of humanity where there is a question regarding the integrity of God to provide us access to what He promised we could become.

TRADING GREATNESS FOR SHAME

The end of all that has been a litany of hiding things from God and others—all because the serpent beguiled Adam into believing that God really cannot be trusted. As he ate, digested and assimilated this newfound food, he began to see those things that made for shame instead of seeing those things that made for greatness. The lens of his inner vision was now shrouded in shame, and it affected his thinking, feeling, doing and speaking. So powerful was the effect of digesting the fruit he had chosen to eat that he became crafty in similar fashion to the serpent.

When Adam heard the sound of God's thunder, his response was to hide. That which used to motivate him now created fear and dread within his soul. He didn't run toward the arrival of the chariots—he ran from them! Adam's dream became his nightmare. He was hiding himself from the presence of the Lord.

The serpent had created an image in the minds of the man and the woman that did not cause any overreaction in them. They believed as the serpent had implied—that darkness and hate motivated this good God.

When the Lord sought Adam out, the question regarding his location was far more about an internal location than a position behind the tree: "Adam, where are you?" The question was tied to Adam's willingness to be transparent. In other words, "Where are you in relationship to Me?" So many issues get shoved down into our souls, somewhere below the level of consciousness, when we succumb to the lie that seduces us.

Adam found it difficult to take responsibility for his choices and his actions in the presence of Truth.

Basically, when Adam said, "I heard the sound of Your approach, and I was naked, so I became afraid and hid," something had become twisted in his perception in relationship to God and the truth. The first question from the Gardener Himself was, "Who told you that you were *naked?*" Then the Lord asked the obvious: "Did you eat from the tree I commanded you not to eat from?"

A WEB OF DECEPTION

Adam's response is renowned—he blamed God and his wife, who in turn blamed the serpent. His inability to take ownership for his choices, his position and his current reality had caused him to suppress the truth in his own soul. Eating of that tree split him on the inside. Death came into his very soul, and he was now without a sense of being joined to the Lord.

That hidden spot is a place of real disconnection. It gets in the way of genuine intimacy and self-disclosure. It's potentially more damaging than the blind spot because it presses things down so deep at an unconscious level that we may not even be able to "get in touch" with the reason we are doing and saying certain things. Without the help of deep, penetrating healing prayer and the searchlight of God's unconditional love, this hidden spot can become so dark and murky that out of its miry clay all manner of uncleanness can begin to manifest.

The serpent hooked Adam and the woman at a feeling

level. The things that were "desirable" imply an emotional hook that anchored them to a spirit of seduction. Their souls became tied up and twisted in a web of deception. They fell into death and darkness.

The innate desire to be "like Daddy" did not leave—instead, it became twisted. They exchanged the true image of the Creator for the false image of the seducer. The seducer promised something he could not deliver by offering an emotional hook to tie up and bind their souls to him.

A LOSS OF IDENTITY

Adam lost his identity. He no longer knew who he was and what he looked like. When the Lord asks, "Who told you that you were naked?" the word used in the Hebrew for *naked* is the same as the root word for *crafty,* which describes the character and nature of the serpent.

This nakedness was, in fact, an exchange of the nature and likeness of God for the deceptive and crafty nature of the serpent. There was a deep loss of a sense of person-hood and humanness in that choice. That one choice led to the fall of the entire human race.

For that reason it is imperative that when we speak of wholeness and healing, we keep in mind that we are not speaking of "self-improvement." Adam lost the true sense of self with which he was created.

Adam lost the reality of his true image, and he became split in the likeness of the tree from which he ate. That tree was a place of making independent judgments as to what was good and what was evil. That was the tree of value judgment. Even now, every time we choose to eat from that tree we experience a sense of death and separation regarding intimacy with the Father. In his translation of Isaiah 30:13, Moffat reads, "Your guilt will split you."

There in that hidden spot lie the patterns of generations and the limiting beliefs of value judgments that prevent us from walking in total unconditional love. Since Adam now had difficulty being able to speak face to face with God in freedom, he was without a mirror to reflect his glory back to him. Adam was clothed in the Garden prior to the fall. He was clothed with glory. Man was made in the image of God's glory. Glory was the covering on the first son of the human race. His glory was given as a gift from the Father of love. Remember that the apostle Paul refers to God the Father in a number of ways:

- The Father of lights
- The Father of spirits
- The Father of glory

Adam's entire being was in the image of God's glory. We cannot know ourselves by ourselves. We can only know ourselves in relation to others, or a significant other, who can reflect and mirror back to us our glory. Consider these words by Thomas Kane:

> Over and above sheer existence, we need to be loved by another human person, *a significant other*. We are given meaning and strength by

the affirmation of our parents, our brothers and sisters, our spouses, our friends, colleagues, and superiors.[2]

When Adam ate of the tree, he fed himself on the outcome of something that produced an independent judgment of what was good and what was evil. *He became less like God and more like the serpent.* There is still so much hiding in that spot deep below the levels of our consciousness. The residue of Adam's nightmare still lives in the broken places in our souls. Even after we experience regeneration, it still takes Spirit-sensitive men and women to become servants of God's healing presence to us in our pain. God has processed these men and women through the crisis of the cross into the greatness of transformation. Having lost the sense of being "good" according to Genesis 1:31, Adam left us a legacy of shame and infirmity. To be *infirmed* is to be made weak. To be *affirmed* is to be made strong and firm. Words indeed pack an emotional punch and create feelings. Affirming words by significant others in our lives are part of the process of healing and wholeness. Unaffirming words by significant others are part of the process of illness and fragmentation.

We have said "peace, peace" where there is no peace, and sadly we have only slightly healed the wound of the people of God. The "quest" for the Father, in a world that is crying out for their absentee fathers—unaffirmed and unaffirming fathers, alcoholic fathers, drug-addicted fathers, workaholic fathers and missing fathers—is beyond comprehension. We all want to be "like daddy."

Our earliest view of life and the world is formed by our relationship to our mother. A baby organizes its world and everything in it in relationship to the face of the mother. That face becomes the baby's security, safety and assurance. A mother's nurturing influence shapes the foundation of our core personality, how we see life and how we see ourselves.

At some point in the process of growth, however, the father or father figure models for us how to be a meaningful partner in our interactions and the intimacies in all our relationships. We define ourselves in the context of our relationships. We do not know ourselves by ourselves. God declared that it was not "good" for man to be alone. Man cannot know himself by himself. In the context of community and meaningful relationships, identity is developed, formed and shaped. In the primary stages the bond between mother and child begins the first phase of that development. A child defines himself or herself in the context of his or her mother.

As we grow and mature, we discover that we can't simply rely on "mama." When we "come of age" and want to find out who we are apart from our mother, our father affirms our awareness that relationships are a matter of choice. It is our father who affirms our growing identity and our sexuality. The older we get and the more we grow up, the more intense our need becomes to find our true identity.

THE BLESSING

We need to know that we are not merely the sons and daughters of our parents. We are looking for the "blessing" that recognizes our true meaning as individuals apart from our parents. We grow from wanting everything to be more and better from Mom and Dad to wanting to be different from them. We find the niche that uniquely belongs to us so that we can fulfill our purpose and destiny.

The patriarchs provided, and still provide, that empowering blessing that sanctions our individuality. The blessing of the father is crucial to the advancement of the next generation.

As we will see later, Jacob and Esau represent a model of the challenges in a family where there is a definite discrepancy in each parent's view of the child—Isaac and Rebekah's differing views of the twins, and a definite competition for the affection of the parent that did not favor them—Jacob for Isaac's affection, and Esau for Rebekah's affection. Dad loved Esau, while mom favored Jacob. Jacob lacked something he desperately needed in the forming of his identity from his father, and Esau lacked something he needed in the forming of his identity from his mother. It caught up to both of them years later, and as a result, each took a unique turn when it came to building his own relationship in marriage and family.

In the remnant of our deep soul the broken image of Adam's legacy sleeps, awaiting a wake-up call from a voice that can summon us to step into greatness. Deep in the memory of Adam lay the youthful dream of innocence in a world gone mad. He now had no way of forming a vision of real maturity and adulthood because his entire world had been changed. His imagination had been defiled by the seductive spirit of the age.

The father of lies had twisted the concept of fatherhood. Adam could no longer forge a dream; he had to live in a nightmare. Adam now moved away from the intimacy of divine presence to the agony of divine absence. Not only was the ground cursed because of this, but also the soil of his own soul became his adversary in seedtime and harvest. The elemental spirits would subject him to their oppressive nature. His own effort and hard labor would lead to a life of blood, sweat and tears.

It would take now the redemptive work of the Father of lights to protect Adam from the harsh reality of the world outside the immediate circle of intimacy in the Garden. There was no "safe place" any longer for Adam to interact with God without the interference of the powers of darkness.

Consider these words from Leanne Payne in her landmark book *The Healing Presence*:

> Separation from the Presence is, quite literally, what the Fall is. As a result of the Fall, mankind slipped from God-consciousness into the hell of self and self-consciousness.
>
> Such a state is at once sinful and incomplete. This fallen self, turned inward and narcissistic, dwells in misconceived feelings and attitudes, those that arise from listening to the self-in-separation and to the voices of a fallen world. That self is to be "put-off"—we are not to practice the presence of that self.... Reckoning ourselves dead to that body of sin in our

members (the old man) and alive to God through Jesus Christ our Lord, we "put on" our new man, the true self (see Romans 6:3–14).[3]

I have come to realize that we are in need of the healing presence of God on an ongoing basis. Recovery and restoration are both process words, and we cannot bypass the process in order to step into greatness. We have all been wounded by the separation that took place in the federal head of the human race, namely Adam.

In Christ we have been redeemed, yet the process of becoming whole, which involves reconnecting with the healing presence and healing voice of the Father, is a journey and takes time. Working through the patterns and images of generations that produce outcomes that exacerbate the absence of God requires a willingness to embrace the process necessary for our souls to be cured and restored. It isn't a one-time shot that cures all our ills. It is a process. Old things pass away in a process; new things emerge out of that process.

GUILT AND HIDING FROM GOD

When Adam ate from the tree of death—the tree of the knowledge of good and evil—his guilt split him on the inside. His head and his heart disconnected. I am convinced that in God's original man there was no split between what he was conscious of and what he was unconscious of. That one fateful choice made by the original man created a gap between the heart and the mind, as well as the conscious and the unconscious.

The Hidden Spot

Original man did not have a hidden spot because, up until that moment, there was nothing to hide. However, after that fateful choice, while his spirit was now separated from God, it still longed for union with God. Yet the taint of deception had now been injected into the veins of humanity and had twisted the means by which to experience the grace for which he longed.

A LOSS OF GLORY

Adam missed the mark and fell from glory. He truly lost his identity, and so he took on the false image of the serpent by now seeking to mask and hide his true identity, which was now marred.

Adam's appearance didn't change. However, his appearance probably lacked the luster it had when the glory was upon him. The glory was removed, and he knew and felt internally that something was missing. He knew he was naked. In place of the glory that was missing, guilt and fear filled the vacancy. Split by independent judgment, he experienced guilt and fear, the outcome (fruit) of the tree of the knowledge of good and evil. He was now quite "unlike" his Daddy, and he couldn't handle it.

Adam had to cover himself with something that was there in the Garden. Something intended to be a blessing to him now became a substitute for glory. Once he picked the leaves from the tree to cover himself, the leaves immediately began to lose their glory as well. It wasn't long before Adam discovered that when you disconnect a leaf from the tree to which it is joined, it loses its glory (its life and reason for being). Death entered creation, and though the leaves looked alive for a while, in no time they withered and dried up, because once separated from their source, they were, for all intents and purposes, dead.

HEALING OUR HIDDEN SPOT

We don't realize how much stuff is dumped into our hidden spot (that we dumped there) until we face the pain of our crisis. Much of our inner dialogue and inner scripting is so deep that we don't even realize what it is we are telling ourselves when we talk to ourselves.

Our feelings, our judgments and our self-sabotaging beliefs live deep in the hidden spot. They pop out every so often like frogs in the mud whenever someone gets too close to the forbidden territory within us. We "croak" in fear and pain whenever anyone steps on the murky soil of our hidden spot. Words and events stir up unconscious reactions in us that are almost "knee-jerk" in their appearance. Someone can say something in total innocence, and our reactions to those words can surprise both them and us.

We may try to recover by saying something like "I didn't mean that"—especially when what comes out of us is the sting of the serpent. *Our need to say "I didn't mean that" is an attempt to hide from others, from God and ultimately from our own unfinished business and ourselves.* We have spewed out something that came "out of nowhere," and we can't take it back. It has already done its damage. There are no mistakes in communication; there are only regrets in the outcomes (fruit) that our communication gives back to us.

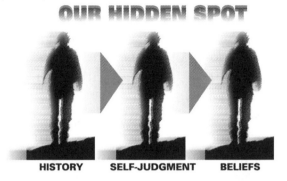

OUR HIDDEN SPOT

HISTORY SELF-JUDGMENT BELIEFS

If we fail to face those three areas in the hidden spot, we cannot erase their effects from our current reality. We find that we keep ourselves up for a repeat performance of what we are trying to avoid. As a result, our hidden spot will become larger and larger.

The hidden spot can create incredible denial when we refuse to experience the painful process of taking a good look at what we are hiding from ourselves, others and God. The closest thing on this side of eternity to "outer darkness," where there is weeping and gnashing of teeth, is the refusal to face the stuff that we ourselves have woven into the layers of our souls by the root judgments we have made concerning our personal history.

Part of the work of the Holy Spirit in our lives is nothing less than the recovery of our souls. The Father of glory will wake us up to understand the patterns of avoidance, rejection, abandonment, manipulation, victimization, seduction, bitterness, regret, despair and the negative emotions that have blocked us from stepping into greatness.

Circumstances do not create our pain. Circumstances merely trigger the pain that is already there, hiding just below the surface of our awareness. The circumstances become a tool in the hand of God to stir up the mud at the bottom of our hidden spot and bring to the surface the judgments, vows and inaccurate beliefs that need to be *released* and then *replaced* with truth, affirmation and unconditional love.

As sons and daughters of Adam, we are living with the consequences of having lost our identities and the essence of our beings. We mask that fact with behaviors that seek to get our needs met by the things we do.

Children who never receive the attention they need may resort to all kinds of inappropriate behaviors in order to get that attention. For them, negative attention is better than no attention at all. Adults who have not dealt with unmet needs for attention in their personal histories will find ways to take revenge on those who they perceive are not meeting their need for such.

The more driven we are by unmet needs, the more we suppress the truth and deepen the hidden spot. As a result, we live less-than-conscious lives, looking awake, but actually sleepwalking through life. Many individuals go through the "motions" of life, drained of the joy of living because they have dumped so much into their hidden spot. They have chosen to survive because living doesn't really seem possible.

Step 1: Becoming reconciled to our history

As the apostle Paul said, it is past time to be awakened out of sleep (Eph. 5:14). It is the intention of the Father to heal the place where darkness has caused us to run and hide.

Stepping into greatness requires that we first reconcile

our personal history so that it no longer hinders access to our destiny. Our personal history cannot change. By the power of God, however, we can gain insight and deliverance from our bitter root judgments, our various other value judgments and our inaccurate beliefs about ourselves, others, our circumstances and God.

Step 2: Asking the Holy Spirit to search us— and show us

A crisis is a defining moment in our life. With the help of the Holy Spirit, our crisis can usher us into a process that will set us free from limitations that have confined us. David cried out for this help in Psalm 139: "Search me, O God, and know my heart; try me and know my anxious thoughts, and *see if there be any hurtful way in me*, and lead me in the everlasting way" (vv. 23–24, emphasis added).

David invited the searchlight of the Holy Spirit to bring things to light that were hiding deep within him. He was not fully aware of *what* they were, but he knew *that* they were. He could *feel* their presence in his heart.

The way we know we have value judgments and that we are value-judging is that we feel disturbed on the inside. If we ignore those feelings long enough, our hearts become hard. Let our hearts become hardened, and our love will grow cold. The result? We will become cynical, suspicious and critical.

Areas exist in all our lives where our "unfinished business" has caught us by surprise when we least expected it. We all need the help of God, the Ultimate Significant Other, and caring significant others to help us sort through the hidden spot.

Step 3: Understanding our history

If we fail to understand our own histories, we can easily sabotage our destinies. It is the intention and will of the Father to bring us from crisis through process into greatness. The key to understanding our history lies in the answers to the following questions. Ask yourself:

1. What memories from your past keep coming up that trouble you?
2. What are you telling yourself at a deep level about those memories?
3. What feelings are associated with those memories?
4. Who were the significant others in your life that truly accepted you unconditionally?
5. Where have you tried to "perform" in order to be accepted?
6. What relationships have you had that have been the most disappointing for you?
7. If you could do it all over, what would you do differently?
8. Who told you that you were "naked"? In other words, what labels stuck to you, formed your identity mask and prevented you from knowing who you truly are? You can substitute any word that comes from your heart and memory as you ask the question again. For example: Who told you that you were shy? Incapable? Incompetent?

9. What feelings have become resident and frozen in your soul, feelings that need to be thawed out?

10. Did anyone ever tell you they believed in you? Who were those individuals?

11. What impact have they made on your life?

12. Where are they now?

Step 4: Preparing ourselves—the process is painful

Are we prepared to engage God and our personal history and face the stuff in the murky and miry clay of our hidden spot? It may bring short-term pain; *however, it will also be followed by long-term pleasure.* If we want to step into greatness, we cannot circumvent the process. There are no shortcuts to wholeness and well-being. The price that was paid by the Son of God included enduring the cross and despising the shame. Shame gets in the way of our future by causing us to hide from our past. Wouldn't you like to get a few steps closer to the greater intention of God for your life? Let's not abort the process now that we are on our way to greatness.

What are you hiding that's eating you alive and preventing you from stepping into greatness?

My own voice—the part of me that is never heard

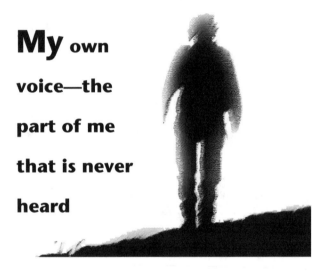

Finding Your Own Voice

It is never too late to be what you might
have been.
—GEORGE ELIOT

WHEN GOD MAKES THE FIRST MOVE TO RECOVER US from our lost estate, His reconciling power has to be applied from the inside out. If I am reconciled to God— and He invites me to be reconciled to Him and His family—how do I do that without being reconciled to those parts of me that I have buried in the dark place called the hidden spot?

Growing up, I so wanted to be like my dad. He was my hero. I didn't get to spend a lot of time "playing" with him though, because he had to run the family business.

His was not a nine-to-five job. He took the business with its entire challenges home with him every night.

MY FATHER'S PLAN

Dad worked very hard to insure my future. His concerns were my grades in school and my health. They were his magnificent obsession as it related to me. He wanted to be sure I was never somewhere that would have threatened my health (where in the world could that have been?). And he wanted to be sure from my very first day at school that I would do well—because I was told I was going to be a doctor.

I have come to understand so much over the years about the reason for those two strong focuses in my dad's life, and I have mellowed in my strong reactions to his overprotection and demands for perfection. While he certainly doesn't have that same drive any longer, it took both of us years to work through the layers of judgments about each other that we had buried deep in our hidden spots.

MY FATHER'S PAIN

As I have already shared, Dad was the oldest son of an Italian immigrant couple who settled in America in the heart of New York City. Against the backdrop of the Great Depression, my grandparents married and raised a large family. They learned how to manage and provide the things that were essential to life. They had faith in God and a dog-eared determination to survive and to build a future for their children.

Dad was about twelve years old when his brother Vito died. Vito was no more than about two and a half years old when the tragedy occurred. My grandmother had intended to scrub the floors. In those days, they would boil hot water on the stove in a large pot and add lye as a cleansing agent. Dad was apparently keeping an eye on his little brother when somehow Vito disappeared into the kitchen and tipped over the hot water and lye. Vito died, and Dad blamed himself.

It was one of those tragic accidents that leave scars on everyone involved. Those scars are embedded in my father's soul, even to this day. I am not sure that he has ever been able to "feel" forgiven and loved in that area of his heart, even though he has done his best to cope with it rationally.

There's that split again: head and heart.

We can intellectually reason with ourselves that we are forgiven, yet experientially never *know* in our hearts the reality of that truth. Value judgments at the tree of death (the tree of the knowledge of good and evil) are not just judgments about God, others and events, but *they are also judgments about ourselves*. The tree of death has produced many things in our total life experience:

- Self-hatred
- Nonconstructive criticism
- Name-calling
- Self-centeredness
- Egotistical behaviors
- Slander

- Gossip
- Envy
- Jealousy
- Backbiting
- Strife
- Manipulation
- Seduction
- Witchcraft and sorcery
- Bitterness and rebellion
- Mental illness

It was quite a high price to pay for Adam to eat the fruit and to assimilate that "knowing" in his conscious and unconscious behaviors and beliefs. We have been paying for it for years.

My dad blamed himself for something that he could not have prevented. As a result, shame became firmly entrenched as part of his identity. You see, we need the Father to reflect and mirror our identity back to us. Our glory is discovered in the reflection of His glory. When we are disconnected from the Father, we leave an opening in our inner garden for the accuser and seducer to come in and usurp God's rightful place and demand our attention (worship). There, in that moment, we exchange the truth of our being for the lie of "doing in order to be," and we bear a false image that hides the real us behind shame.

Not only has Dad had difficulty accepting God's forgiveness, but he has also had a hard time forgiving himself. He has carried Vito and watched over him, though he is in heaven, for years and years. The significance of that value judgment in Dad caused him to adopt certain patterns of behavior in relationship to his only son that created challenges for me that only increased as I got older.

Much of his "over concern" about not wanting me to catch a cold, get sick or get hurt and his careful consideration of my need for rest were merely attempts to make sure he never failed to watch out for someone again, especially his own child. That I was his only child only compounded his concern. My dad's way of freeing himself from the pain of his brother's death, and his shame in not preventing it, was to try and make up for the loss of his brother.

TRANSFERRED DREAMS

All I ever wanted growing up was to please my dad. In the earlier years, I never questioned his concerns about my health or my schoolwork. I figured all parents had those same expectations and concerns for their kids. I was going to be a doctor, and one of the ways that was going to happen was that I was going to be in the doctor's office for every little sniffle.

By the time I reached adolescence, I began to react to Dad's need to overprotect and direct me. I still wanted to be like Dad, and I wanted his affirmation more than ever—but I discovered that I couldn't always live up to his expectations. I began to resist his demands, and we began to conflict in many ways. My will was as strong as his will, so I added to the premature graying in my dad's hair.

As I grew older I began to ask a great deal of questions:

- Why do I need to become a doctor?
- Why do you want me to be a doctor?
- Why didn't you become a doctor?

Dad was determined I was going to medical school. It was drummed into me from infancy. I found out at a certain point in time that Dad was in college in a pre-medical program for two years and then had to serve time in the army during World War II.

When he returned home after the war was over, he was in his mid-twenties and felt he was too old to go back to finish his premed training and then go to medical school. But the real reason was more complicated. The war took something out of him, and for some reason he lost his will to pursue medicine. Seeing the pain and the capability of destruction in humanity had a profound effect on Dad's psyche. My dad didn't lay his dream aside so much as he transferred it—to me.

Dad wanted me to be what he never was able to be. As much as I wanted to be like my dad, the older I got, the less I fit into his dream for the future. I was torn by the desire to be like Dad and the quest to find my own identity. *I began to feel as though the life I was being asked to live was not the life I was born to live.*

Yet always in the midst of the inner conflict and the outer confrontations there was a deep longing for my dad's approval. I took the lack of approval as an indication of my inadequacy in not being able to live up to what I was supposed to be. I learned how to "perform" for approval so effectively that it bled into every area of my life.

In order to cope and survive the turmoil, I masked

many of my real feelings and buried them deep inside. I lived with a great deal of fear. I was fearful of rejection, disapproval, being invisible and being forgotten and left out. I felt as though there was no room for me to be myself. What was worse, I didn't really know who I was.

THE GREATEST GIFT

The greatest gift I believe we can give our children is peace of mind from a very early age. God promised that we would be led forth in peace (Isa. 55:12). Training up a child in the path toward intended destiny cannot take place if we fail to take into account the internal map they arrived with from God. This internal map has the intention and direction of God already written on it. While Adam's race is fallen, and the image of glory has been defaced, there remains the signature of God on every individual soul. Built by God to fulfill specific and intentional purpose, the cry for genuine greatness lies deep at the core of our human experience.

If that cry is unheard and that core criterion unaffirmed, the child might never grow to become who he or she was meant to be. Those energies will be directed in other less productive—and sometimes even destructive—ways as he seeks to fill the void within him by creating meaning in things that promise much, yet deliver little.

Dad's need to relive his life in his son was tied to unfulfilled dreams. I now understand that in moments when my behaviors touched the pain in his own heart, he reacted to me with language that was the shame-based self-talk of his own soul. He kept burying his pain deep in the dark places of his hidden spot by reacting to my refusal to comply with his demands. *Little did Dad realize that he was modeling a way of life for me.*

I continued to bury my pain and disown my own feelings. Yet in doing this, I only succeeded in perpetuating my own fears and anxieties. Firmly rooted in bitterness, my self-talk revolved around the fears of failure and rejection. I was consumed with my own pain, and I had to hide my feelings from my father because I knew he would reject me if I opened up and told the truth. So I made it through those years by burying my feelings and masking my behaviors.

I withdrew a whole lot. I struggled with feeling as though I didn't fit in even with the friends with whom I grew up. Since my performance was tantamount to acceptance, I often faced the fact that my performance was never quite good enough. I lived a life of constant comparison and competition.

I pressured myself to keep getting better; I had to do at least as well as others—if not better. I was awkward in so many areas. I lacked the coping skills and language skills that could have served me well in my earlier years.

We didn't handle feelings well in our family, so we buried them. We hid behind our own fig leaves out of the shame of not knowing who we were anymore. We didn't affirm one another—we blamed one another. We demanded things from each other.

I can remember nights of almost total silence when things weren't going well for Dad in the family business. If I brought home a report card that was less than his expectation, it got pretty intense at the dinner table.

Then there was a long period of silence that often would last for days. By the time I was in my late teens, I was convinced that nothing I ever did was going to be good enough, so I cast off the restraints and rebelled as much as possible. I was angry, confused, uncertain and quite unaffirmed.

THE QUEST FOR THE BLESSING

When we are afraid of rejection, we hide in more ways than one. The hidden spot is tied to the need for forgiveness, healing and restoration, as well as affirmation. I have often reflected on the hidden spot in my own life and considered the story of Jacob and his father, Isaac.

At the end of his life, when it came time for Isaac to pass on the blessing, he was already incapable of seeing well. In order to obtain the blessing that Isaac intended for Esau, Jacob hid under the skin of a goat and went to his frail and dying father, pretending to be Esau. It was his mother's idea.

The tragedy in the family of Isaac dated back a long way. While the twins were in their mother's womb, God revealed that the younger was the heir of the birthright. God was going to change the rules of blessing. The unloved son was to be the heir. Certainly Rebekah informed Isaac of that fact. Yet when the children were born, it was Esau who won his father's heart. Esau was Isaac's favorite.

Have you ever considered what might be the reason that Isaac favored the son who had a taste for game and liked the wilderness and hunting? Consider Isaac's own childhood. When he was born, his father, Abraham, was already an old man. Isaac's brother Ishmael was a hunter and had a wild streak in him. Abraham loved Ishmael. Little boys want to please their dads. Isaac was no exception. Is it possible that Isaac saw what Abraham loved about Ishmael? Perhaps he wished he could be like his older brother so that his dad would be pleased.

Something had to be deeply scripted in Isaac's soul for him to reject the Lord's word regarding the twins and choose to honor what he *preferred* over what God had *declared*. Jacob wasn't what Isaac thought a son should be, ought to be or must be. *Shoulds, oughts* and *musts* become the "letter of the law" that is impossible to fulfill. Jacob was the complete antithesis of what Isaac's "image" of a son was. Jacob was unloved, unaffirmed and unseen by his father.

While in his old age Isaac couldn't see well, he never saw Jacob well *ever*. He didn't merely fail to recognize him in the tent under the goatskins and the speech of performance. He was incapable of seeing in his son what he saw so well in himself.

Isaac wanted a son that was like his big brother, Ishmael, because he saw how much Ishmael gave pleasure to *his* father. The closest thing in Isaac's future that related to the stuff hidden in his past was Esau.

Although Jacob "performed" as Esau, his voice could not be changed. We can hide certain aspects of ourselves from others, yet our voices will give us away every time. Fear will register in our voice even if we are masking it. Displeasure will register in our voice even if we are smiling and saying the opposite of what we really feel to the person with whom we are talking. If that person is sensitive and in touch with his current reality, he will be able to hear our voice behind the performance. The hands may be the hands of Esau, yet the voice will be the voice of Jacob.

I studied carefully what seemed to get my dad's attention and affirmation in our extended family. I began to compare myself with my cousins when my Dad made a fuss over their grades and other accomplishments. I was never quite able to match their accomplishments, but I became fiercely competitive in an effort to compensate for the pain of not feeling affirmed. Since I was never "good enough" (which was a great deal of my inner dialogue), I just kept trying harder. However, it didn't help me. It just made the pain that much more solidified within me.

In that hidden spot there can be so much buried pain stored up, only to flood forth years down the road when we no longer can hide from ourselves. My "flood" came when I was already overwhelmed. Reeling from the pain of betrayal and overwhelmed by a sense that I should have been farther along than I was, out of the blue my spirit began to spew forth a deluge of pain and disappointment.

I had learned to mask so well that I became numb to the pain I was hiding. Flashbacks of incidents and memories flooded my mind, and I was feeling weak and undone. I began to weep and didn't know why.

In retrospect, I realize that I was at a turning point in my journey. The awakening process that culminated in a refining led to a defining moment that was just beginning. Sometimes we can bury things so deeply that vows and judgments we have made hold us in prison for a long time and prevent us from accessing the doorway that leads to the greatness for which we were created.

SABOTAGING RELATIONSHIPS

I learned how to remain aloof by observing my dad's reactions to situations. He was far more closed than open when I was growing up. As a child, I didn't quite understand it. Yet, as I grew and watched him process his own journey, I gained some insight into his behavior. Little did I realize that those conclusions would eventually catch up with me.

I had learned to interpret any question from him, and later from everyone else, as resistance to my point of view. It never dawned on me that some people genuinely sought clarification and were not questioning my premises. I had developed a learned response from relating to an authoritarian father who had many things to teach me that were proper and true. Yet, whenever I asked for clarification from him, I usually received a defensive response. Eventually I adopted his behaviors.

Another part of me, however, remained quite people-oriented. I feared the loss of approval in my social relationships. Inside of me were a need to remain aloof and distant and a need to connect with others. I couldn't quite sort out those two seemingly polar opposites. Both were born out of the same need for being affirmed for who I was, as opposed to being affirmed for whom someone else wanted me to be.

When we are all in knots on the inside, communication can become challenging. Out of touch with our own feelings, we are unaware of the feelings our words and actions create in others around us.

Words create feelings. Feelings touch people at many levels. I needed to be in control of all my emotions, to the degree that I wasn't honest with them all the time. I wanted to be as sincere as I knew how to be, yet I also had this awareness of just how much of a "bottom-line" person I was. I wrestled with the critical, judgmental part of me that was "just like Dad." I was afraid of letting people know what I really felt, because I did not have the skill to describe what I was feeling without venting. I was also afraid of the results I would get if I vented. As a kid, I vented when some bigger guys would pick on me because I was small. Generally, it cost me a few bruises.

The schoolyard I hung out in as a kid was a great place, yet it was also a tough place. Many of the kids in the neighborhood were street smart with "chips" on their shoulders. If the need to vent my emotions got the best of me, I might find myself, as I did on two occasions, reacting to guys who were twice my size. It didn't take much to provoke them, even without meaning to do so. I had my share of close calls, which only reinforced my need to keep a lid on my feelings and frustrations.

Dad had a pretty short fuse and was rather low on empathy when it came to my imperfect performance, as measured against the standard he had set for me. The seeds of resistance sprouted and grew in my spirit, and the judgments and vows I made took me to some challenging places later on down the road.

FACING REGRET

My refining crisis forced me to revisit many of these long-held beliefs and behaviors. That question—"Shouldn't you be farther along by now?"—kept coming up. The emotional content of that question was powerful. Many of us have wrestled with it from time to time.

It is none other than regret.

Regret can be a thief that steals our present moment by locking us into our past disappointments. It sabotages our hope for moving into the future. Regret blinds us to what is taking place in the now. Regret weighs us down. It causes us to rehash our mistakes endlessly in a nonproductive manner.

When we have to be perfect, there is no room for mistakes. Every mistake we make adds to the weight of regret we carry in our memory bank and our emotional vault.

Whose life script are you playing out, yours or someone else's?

THE PROCESS
THAT SHAPES YOU

The

hallway to

greatness—

the nowhere

between two

somewheres

Unpacking Your Bags

Education mainly consists of what we
have unlearned.
— MARK TWAIN

WE CARRY A GREAT DEAL OF EXCESS BAGGAGE WITH US
from our past, yet we fail to realize it until we find ourselves facing the defining moment of a refining crisis.

I often say that I was built for comfort, because I
really dislike conflict. This is because the conflicts that
took place at home when I was growing up rarely
seemed to lead to peaceful resolutions. If conflict didn't
lead to a peaceful resolution, it didn't pay to enter the
conflict—at least in my boyhood home.

I have had to learn the less-than-easy way that at

times conflict has to do with fighting for what has been entrusted to us as a steward by God. Others may seek to usurp our stewardship by a spirit of entitlement and justify their unbecoming behaviors in an effort to sabotage our efforts. But this is because of their own unfinished business and their hidden spot.

The creative tension between destiny and fate comes into place when we fail to confront our hidden spot. What goes around comes around, and God allows life to give us back what we are dishing out until we are willing to break the patterns that have been ingrained in us. Facing those patterns and discovering what keeps popping up from our past is like unpacking our bags at the end of a trip.

THE ART OF UNPACKING

I travel often and have done so for years. I am used to the rhythm of early morning flights and hotel rooms, although I don't relish them. They are part of those necessary things that come with the stewardship given to me from God.

Years ago, when I first began to travel, I would take everything except the kitchen sink. They say women are notorious for overpacking. Well, I was far more zealous about overpacking than my wife was in those days. I packed based on the fear of not having what I needed when I arrived.

Some concern about not having what is needed is acceptable. However, taking three of the same item for a one-day or two-day trip was extreme. It slowed down my movement from airports to hotels and back again. It got old after a while—a *short* while.

I had to begin to pack consciously and not allow my fears to determine the weight I would carry into the place I was headed. There is an art to packing, and there is also an art to unpacking. There came a point where I discovered by experience that many of the things I brought were never worn or used on the road; they just took up space in my suitcase and in the closet of the hotel room. We hang onto things that we think we need but are not necessary because of fears in our lives from our past.

ENTERING THE HALLWAY

Somewhere between the refining crisis and the opportunity to step into greatness there is a place we are asked to enter and experience. It is the "hallway" to which I have been referring. It is the place between our *former* somewhere and our *future* somewhere. What gets us to the door of the hallway is the crisis. Something touches our life that upsets our status quo—something that we thought would last forever changes in a moment.

We live in a fast-paced information age where job shifting and job downsizing have become a way of life. People are moved around more in one lifetime than previous generations ever moved at all. Things can change so rapidly that there is no time to bring closure to the chapters of our lives. We are here today and somewhere else tomorrow. This rapid pace robs us of the ability to process and grieve—to recognize endings and embrace new beginnings.

The doorway to the hallway that leads to greatness is

opened by grief. Grief is what permits us to move on. Something we thought would last forever comes to an end. We didn't see it coming, and it came without our permission. *Maybe we didn't want to see it coming.* Or perhaps others tried to protect us from what they knew was coming—they chose to believe we could not handle it if we knew the truth. We can even find ourselves compensating for one another's hidden spots and blind spots. We may also come to premature conclusions about things that are not quite as accurate as we thought.

When a relationship ends, whether by mutual consent, betrayal, sharp disagreement or dying, it feels like death. Something is taken away upon which we relied. Even if the relationship was not what we expected it to be, there is still a loss involved.

We have to let go of something and admit that it is gone. If we don't want to accept an ending, our first tendency is to deny it even took place. If we stay in denial long enough, we set ourselves up for far greater pain in a future backwash for which we definitely won't be ready.

Unpacking our bags when something is over can be difficult. Once, when I spent thirty days in Germany, Switzerland and Austria, I had collected so many memories and notes from people that upon returning home I found it difficult to unpack my bags. If I unpacked my bags, I would have had to admit the trip was over. As long as the suitcase was still packed, I could feel as if I were still "just getting back" with plenty of time to unpack.

A grieving widow may find it difficult to give away those things that are hanging in her husband's closet, sitting on the back porch or sitting on the shelves of the garage. Every place she looks, reminders refresh what once was and no longer is. We can cherish the memory, but it isn't healthy to get stuck in the past. Getting stuck in the past can cause us to fail to accept the present and stall the future.

Many nights I mulled over in my mind occasions I had spent over the years with someone I thought to be true and genuine. All the words, all the right phrases, all the appearance of loyalty were included in the package. It was radically disorienting and shocking to discover I never knew the real person.

I went back in my memory over dinners, picnics, trips to the movies and trips around the country. I found myself quivering and shaking at the stark reality of discovering it was all a mask. It was all a charade.

Deep feelings of anger mixed with sadness would erupt out of nowhere, and I found myself numb from the pain of it all. Stories began to emerge from person after person of their experiences with me and the perceptions they had of me. I remember coming to a point where I just couldn't bear to hear anymore. So much damage had been done that even if I tried to present the truth, there was no longer the ability for some to listen.

There came moments when I experienced deep and profound isolation. I felt very much "cut off from the land of the living." While I was at one level grateful that I had some answers for things that went awry for no apparent reason, at another level I wondered where God was in all the mess. I felt estranged from God, disconnected from my core passion and out of sync with destiny.

In this moment of grieving and pain, the hallway to greatness was before me. But I was carrying too many things to enter it. Unpacking and unloading everything that I had accumulated in terms of emotional baggage took some time. I didn't realize how much I had from previous journeys that I had never unpacked.

In the hallway we begin to dump all the excess baggage and cargo that we have been carrying. We discover how much we adopted from others that was not our opinion or belief as much as it was what someone else wanted us to believe. We experience great upheaval in the hallway because we find ourselves being invited to become true to whom God made us to be.

NARROW IS THE WAY

To enter the hallway of process, I needed to take only those things that would fit through the door. The hallway in the process tends to be a narrow place. Jesus said, "The way is narrow that leads to life" (Matt. 7:14). I didn't realize how much unpacking I needed to do in order to make it through the hallway. Carrying unnecessary burdens can prevent us from experiencing all the things that God has in store for us. Extra weight slows us down and limits our choices.

The hallway is a tight place, and within its corridors we are invited to embrace a disorienting process of letting go of what was once familiar. Once we pass through the exit door of our *crisis* and enter into the hallway of *process*, God sees to it that the door closes behind us. It becomes difficult to turn back.

When a refining crisis touches our lives and there is

an ending to what was once familiar, the first thing we do is to try to take some of the familiar things with us into the process. We also try to turn around and go back through the door from where we just came.

And for good reason. That hallway can be the low place David went through where he had to face his dark shadows: "Yea, though I walk through the [hallway of shadows]..." (Ps. 23:4, KJV). The path is in a valley, a low place in the terrain of our lives as well as our souls. It is a place where the ego is weaned from all its former attachments. We begin to face the dark shadows of the false images and masks that have become routine behaviors that are no longer on the "acceptable list" if we are to truly step into greatness.

God allows us to experience the dark side of our inner life. For some, this can be the "dark night of the soul" of which the early church fathers often spoke. For others, it can be a season of radical disorientation and displacement where nothing seems to fit anymore.

In the hallway we are invited not only to look at our masking behaviors, but also to discover that all the wonderful things we wanted to see take place in our lives no longer have an appeal. It is one thing to be set free from selfish ambition—it is another to find that we no longer even have what it takes to embrace those redeemed and godly ambitions that were such a part of our dreams and desires at one time. This is the place of total detachment. We may even feel as if God isn't with us in the hallway.

We are totally in the dark, and we can't see where we are going. We have to grope and feel our way through the hallway. All sorts of emotions rise up inside us in that dark place—anxiety, dread of the future, low-grade frustration, high-grade anger, sadness, despair and everything in-between.

It seems almost paradoxical that the Father invites us to embrace a vision of an enlarged future and then the Spirit precipitates a crisis equal to what it will take in our personal lives to get us moving toward it. Then at the moment we least expect it, we walk through the crisis exit door. We expect to have our feet set in a large place, only to discover that on the other side of the door is the most uncomfortable and tight place we have ever been.

We expect enlargement, only to meet confinement. We expect a broad pathway, only to discover a narrow walkway. We find that there is no room in this process for any baggage. That long, dark and narrow place looks as if it will destroy us, but it is actually designed to build us. What appears to diminish us is actually the tool of God to increase us. Those forces in our life intended to intimidate us are seen for what they are: shadows that cannot hurt us once we see them for ourselves. There in the hallway we may be disillusioned—that is, stripped of our illusions. But in their place we will also catch a glimpse of a true vision of the person we can become in God, the person He truly made us to be.

I had to come to terms with all the value judgments I had made about myself, others, my world and even God. I had to "unpack" all those judgments and then pay attention to how subtly that tendency could creep right back up on me when I least expected it.

Jesus made it clear that we were to "judge not," and I was becoming aware of how much I wasn't listening to the healing voice of the Father or the voice of the new man inside me. I had the residue of Adam's nightmare, the memory of the old man still lingering in my soul. His illusions were fueled by the voices of the world. They were robbing me of the ecstasy of living a totally affirming lifestyle, one in which I could actually begin to live in the "judge not" about which Jesus admonished us.

The exquisite outcomes that were awaiting me after I began to reconcile my personal history would prove to be incredibly wonderful and overwhelmingly abundant.

What inside of you is hindering you from unpacking your bags?

The hallway to greatness—the healing place where you are reconciled to your history

7

Making Sense of Where You've Been

Never let yesterday use up too much of
today.

—Kobi Yamamda

Life is a series of connections with our future and
destiny in God. Connecting on the inside with God and
with our true identity paves the way for connecting on
the outside with the unfolding order the Father has prepared. There, destiny and opportunity meet, and the
Spirit invites us to step into greatness.

In order to connect with our destiny, we must first
revisit and understand our history. And understanding

is only the first step. Once we understand our inaccurate beliefs, judgments and points of view, we must surrender them to the Holy Spirit. When we do this, He sends renewal, enlargement, wholeness and well-being.

The "hallway" between crisis and destiny is the place where it all gets sorted out. The hallway is that uncomfortable weigh station between our history and our destiny. It is the place where God takes us through the process of revealing and healing our history. It is the place where our history becomes the stepping stone to our destiny, not the derailer and disqualifier of our destiny.

What, then, is the way through this place of transition? If we feel that we are at an all-time low in the hallway, how do we find the stamina and strength to choose to move forward and hang in there, no matter what?

The crisis drew more attention after it was over, and I wasn't prepared for that. We spent so many months "unraveling" things and trying to detangle things that it became a consuming issue. All the while it became clear that God was unraveling *me*.

God was endeavoring to *redefine* my place and my identity in relation to His purpose, yet I felt that I was in the dark about it all. Things were changing all around me as well as within me. For one thing, I didn't know at the time that unpacking my spiritual bags included letting go of some one-way relationships that were dragging me away from God's intentions. During this time, it felt as if my introduction to all the new things God had for me was by the separation from the old things.

God invited me to look at all my relationships and to consider my reasons for being in them. That was tough, and I wasn't sure I wanted to answer some of those questions for myself. I still had within me a deep need to belong. This in and of itself is not a problem—unless it becomes something that gets in the way of our greater purpose.

I was desperate to get a handle on what was taking place here in the hallway. I felt I could cooperate with where God was going. But it seemed that the farther into the hallway I traveled, the less of a clue I had as to what was taking place. The hallway was darker than ever—impenetrable darkness. Emotionally, I had hit rock bottom.

I wanted God to show up and make things clear. Well, He didn't—at least not at that moment and certainly not to my satisfaction. Later there would come a very poignant and moving encounter with the Spirit of the Lord, yet for now I was at the midpoint in the process— and the sense of aloneness was overpowering. I was moving away from the crisis, yet I was not close enough to step into greatness.

THE NEED FOR APPROVAL

I often overcompensated for growing up without siblings by making lots of friends. I *had* to connect with absolutely as many people as I could. I *needed* to make connections. The hunger in me for relationship drove me to make sure I went out of my way to get to know people—not just for belonging, but for *approval.*

I told myself that God was calling me to be part of a

certain group of people as part of His purpose and destiny for my life. But what was actually driving me was my unmet need for acceptance.

It seemed that the more I tried to fit in, the more invalidated I was as a person. My need for approval had enmeshed me in a series of one-sided relationships. I always took the initiative to make contact. They always criticized me—and I always believed it. I was being made to play the fool, and I was the last to recognize it. All I could think was, *What's wrong with me?*

Because I was out of touch with my own inner drive, I missed many of the nonverbal signals that others were giving off. Missing those signals made room for the shock and crisis of betrayal—but it also became the wake-up call for a new future. I was out of touch with my own feelings, so it was very difficult to discern what was going on at a feeling level in others. *You cannot truly connect at a deep level with someone else if you are disconnected from your own self emotionally.*

I never paused to consider how it felt to be a part of this group. How did it feel to be routinely invalidated? How did it feel to be repeatedly criticized? How did it feel to make gestures of friendship that were seldom reciprocated? How did it feel to be an object of ridicule?

Well, in a word it felt *terrible*. And working so hard for approval made me weary beyond words.

There were many times over the years that my true friends tried to explain to me what these relationships were doing to me. But I couldn't receive their loving counsel—not because I didn't want to, but because I so wanted to connect. I just couldn't see what they were talking about.

And so I felt the need to protect and defend the very people who really couldn't have cared less about me. I was not only defensive because I couldn't discern the larger picture, but I was also defensive because *I* was the one who made the decision to seek out these people as friends.

When my wife (who is my best friend) would try to help me see what was going on, I would feel this intense anxiety overtake me, gripping my head and my stomach. It would paralyze me, and I would react in frustration. Having been through the hallway of process, I have come to understand some things about what happens when feelings of anxiety come. Anxiety is a "fusing together" of feelings, memories, thoughts and speculations that are so tangled that we don't want to take the time to sort them out.

Yet at that dark midpoint in the hallway, God was searching my heart and confronting me about what I had been doing for most of my life to "fit in." I found myself unconsciously withdrawing from many things that involved me in one-way relationships. I was hiding from people. I was rearranging my schedule to do so by canceling speaking engagements and even not showing up at board meetings. *Something was taking place inside me.*

I still had a deep desire to connect, yet I was moving away from the pattern of how I built relationships. As painful as some of the separations were, this was also a time where God was inviting me to leave behind performance-driven relationships.

There in the middle of the hallway, as I left behind performance-based living, I discovered that there was no longer a drive to do certain things in order to preserve or maintain my one-sided relationships. As time went on, I became more peaceful as the emotional thunderstorms ended.

I found that solitude provided an incredible backdrop for a more relaxed view of where life and God were taking me. There at the midpoint in the hallway, at its darkest spot, a new identity began to take shape—and I wasn't even aware of what was taking place at first.

I have come to realize that all of this is essential in the process of transformation. In actual fact, we are *always becoming and never arriving*. The upward call is to never stop moving and to never stop changing. We are to move from one level of glory to another. In between each level of glory we experience a lull, a low place. In actual fact, it is as much a gift as the high places.

HEALING OUR HISTORY

There in that low place we come to rely on the *rod and the staff*, which become God's tangible and touchable means of bringing us through the process. For the sons of Abraham, the staff was both the indication of their calling as travelers and shepherds and the instrument by which they preserved their history for the generations to come. The Israelites inscribed their history on the tribal staff and the family staff. Each Israelite had a staff in his hand. Etched on each staff would be notches and symbols describing significant events in their lives.

For Moses, the staff was what he leaned on for forty years in the wilderness when the winds of change drove him far from the people he loved. When he encountered God at Horeb, God commissioned him to walk into his destiny. But at that point, Moses had more questions than faith. God responded to his questions—but then posed one of His own: "What is that in your hand?" Moses responded that it was his staff. It was all he carried with him on his trip through the desert. He looked as if he were traveling light. He seemed to be carrying nothing with him from Egypt—but was that really the case? God commanded Moses to cast his staff to the ground. When he did, God instantly transformed it into a venomous serpent. This terrified Moses, and it would probably have terrified us as well. But was there more to Moses' terror than the simple instinctive fear of a snake?

Our remembrance of the past and our personal history can be tough to look at—especially if we don't want to admit from where we have come. Moses was pretty sure he knew what he had in his hand, but God knew better. God wasn't performing a magic act for Moses. *Rather, God was showing this man of destiny that his unfinished business was getting ready to bite back if Moses didn't get a handle on it.*

The serpent occupies a unique place in the imagery and symbolism of Holy Writ. We know, of course, that the serpent was the instrument used by the powers of darkness to entice the original man and woman to break covenant with God. Jesus admonished His disciples that they were to be *as wise as serpents* and as harmless as doves. The great Pharaoh wore a gold-coiled serpent as his headdress when he sat enthroned in Egypt.

105

Moses was born a Hebrew and raised an Egyptian. *The greatest challenge for Moses was to reconcile his own personal history in the context of his greater purpose in destiny.* That snake represented that part of his past that he had tried to bury in the sand with the Egyptian he had smitten. When Moses killed the Egyptian, he was in some way destroying a part of himself. He could not reconcile his Egyptian upbringing until God invited him to face the part of his life that he was fleeing. For it was precisely that part of his history that was truly essential to where he was going. In order to out-strategize Pharaoh, it was essential to know how he thought, felt and reacted. *It took a Hebrew raised as an Egyptian to deliver the Hebrews that were enslaved by the Egyptians.*

Moses needed to get a handle on his history (staff) so that it could be truly incorporated into his destiny. In that moment when he picked up the serpent by its tail and it turned back into a staff, he "backed into" that part of his history he had not been able to face head-on before. *Now he was ready to let his history work for him instead of against him.* Personal history becomes a comfort to our lives once God reconciles us to it and it to us. When we are in the hallway, God will provide us an opportunity to see our past more clearly so that we can stop running from it and get a handle on it.

POINTED TO A SHINING FUTURE

Once the staff was back in his hand, Moses then pointed it in the direction of the future. That staff is referred to as a rod every time it is pointed in the direction of the future.

Once we are reconciled to our personal history, there is power to move into our inherent destiny. The rod of the future and the staff of the past provide comfort in the hallway, which is the midpoint between my history and my destiny. There at that strategic point between where I have come from and where I am going, the comfort of God is found in the reconciled remembrance of what the root cause of my past crisis actually was.

As I let go of the way I had approached relationships in my history, all that painful history regarding relationships became rich in meaning. My past could now teach me about my future. All learning is by trial and error. I now understood my mistakes—not as an indication of failure, but rather as a valuable source of feedback on my journey. I began to be free to form healthy friendships for healthy reasons.

SEEING THINGS AS THEY REALLY ARE

In the hallway God will cause us to revisit our past and confront our inaccurate beliefs, judgments and points of view. He will invite us to yield to His Spirit for the experience of renewal, enlargement, wholeness and well-being.

For our destiny (rod) and our history (staff) to become the means of God's comfort in the hallway, we need to see our history for what it really is. Like the staff in the hand of Moses, while our history may look strong and straight, our history is not as it appears. When he cast down his staff in God's presence, he discovered that what he thought was straight was actually serpentine and terrifying—and so is your history until it is revisited.

The serpent was that part of his own Egyptian history that had to become integrated and reconciled to his destiny. His "serpentine" past needed first to be seen for what it was and then for how he had been affected by it. In the case of Moses, the effect was profound, for he spent forty years in the hallway doing nothing more than running away from himself.

Getting a handle on the serpentine thing in his past was the key to being empowered by the Spirit to untwist others who were wrapped up in their own unreconciled past. The staff of his history then became powerful enough to swallow up other Egyptian serpentine staffs that were challenging his right to the true freedom that was his destiny.

If you could rewrite your history, would you?

The hallway to greatness— the place where destiny begins to awaken

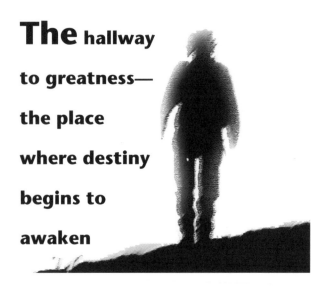

Arriving at the Breakpoint

To every person there comes that special moment when he is tapped on the shoulder to do a very special thing unique to him. What a tragedy if that moment finds him unprepared for the work that would be his finest hour.
—Winston Churchill

The light of the body is the eye. Real illumination is not a sixty-watt bulb in the ceiling—it is the light of the truth in our innermost being. There in that deep innermost place, the most unknown place in our lives, lie the hidden treasures of the kingdom of God—the

Christ in us who is the hope of glory. When light rises from inside our inner man, our footsteps are made firm, and our journey to the end of the hallway becomes more accessible.

When the light goes on inside of us, we become more aware of the reasons for our behaviors. In addition, we begin to understand our drives to get our unmet needs fulfilled. We are being set free from the confining limitations that have been culturally, socially, deceptively, demonically and personally imposed on our life. We begin to see the power behind the events that has gotten us into difficulty and prevented us from being able to accurately define our current reality.

The destiny of God is woven into the fabric and fiber of our souls. We bear the imprimatur of the Father on our hearts. When we arrive at the breakpoint, we will experience the part of the process of which the wake-up call of our crisis intended to make us conscious. We are brought face to face with where we are not like the One in whose image and likeness we were made. *There in that breakpoint I do not merely see God. I see me.*

SEEING IN THE LIGHT OF HIS LIGHT

I have traveled for years and have spent as much time in hotels as I have in my own home. The lighting in most hotel bathrooms is quite different than the lighting in our personal bathrooms. The bathroom mirror in my house has some very elegant looking light fixtures to enhance the ambience of the room. Yet the lights in those pretty fixtures are nothing more than forty-watt bulbs. They give off enough light to see what I am doing.

They don't give off enough light to see what I *really* look like. I like the lighting in my bathroom, because when I gaze into the mirror there, I remain quite comfortable with what I see.

However, in most of the hotels in which I stay while on the road, there are bright white fluorescent lights in the bathrooms. I see a whole lot more of me that I didn't know was there, and I don't necessarily like what those bright white fluorescent bulbs show me about myself.

At the breakpoint in the hallway, when the light in me is seen as darkness, I am invited to see light in God's light. There I move from being comfortable about what I see in the forty-watt light of my own spirit to the incredible white light of His glory. No matter how we look at it, it can be quite threatening to our sense of equilibrium. We certainly will say, "Woe is me, for I am undone." Being "undone" in the presence of God is both wonderful and frightening at the same time.

As we see ourselves in His light, we want to remove those things that have squeezed Him out and prevented His love from flowing to us and through us. There our heart and head experience the beginning of genuine metamorphosis.

Transformation requires renewal, or the making new again of something that got old and worn out. Renewal requires the Greek word *metanoia*, which we have come to know as repentance. I became convinced in the hallway that if destiny were to unfold, I needed to make a fundamental shift in my thinking and perception of God, my world and myself. Once I am "undone," I am ready to be "redone."

WALKING IN THE LIGHT

If I walk in the light, as God is in the light, I can then connect with others in the light. If the light that has been in me is unclear because my "eye is not clear," then distortion becomes the filter through which I perceive reality. When I have not discerned where I am and why I am doing what I'm doing, I cannot be made whole.

I cannot be made whole without a context of community. When Jesus quoted this proverb in Luke 4:23, "Physician, heal yourself," He was underscoring the truth that there can be no wholeness apart from community. But there is a difference between a community and the people who happen to live around you.

The hometown rabble in Nazareth proved to be the polar opposite of a community for Jesus. They believed that He "owed" them something. They minimized Him by saying things that were sarcastic and biting. They tried to mow Him down to their own size: "Isn't this the carpenter's son?" (See Mark 6:3.) They saw Him in the dimmed light of their own flawed understanding.

They demanded healing, yet they did not see themselves as needing what He had to offer. They saw "others" in their community as less fortunate, while they saw themselves as not in need at all. They also felt that if He were truly a prophet, He should at least pay His respects to what they did to help shape His reality.

SEPARATION FROM TOXIC RELATIONSHIPS

The path to greatness through the hallway of process often leads to separation from toxic relationships. The way those relationships generally end is similar to what happened to Jesus when He returned home. He discerned their lack of ability to see Him for who He was and, therefore, their inability to affirm Him for who He was. Yet they had heard about what He had *done*.

They were out of touch with His *being*, yet they were very interested in His *doing*. They wanted Him to validate Himself by performing in their midst. Sadly He could not perform many miracles there, because they refused to accept His true identity. They did not believe *in* His identity; they believed *against* His identity and were demanding "proof" of it before they would believe.

BECOMING AWAKE

Unaffirmed, we can remain slaves to the opinions and demands of others. When God turns on the light and arouses us out of sleep, the "limbs" of our spiritual selves on which we have been sleeping begin to "tingle" as the blood begins to flow into those parts that have been inactive. When our wake-up call comes and our affirmation from the Father is received, we begin to *feel* in places where we previously had no feelings.

As I child, and even now sometimes as an adult, I have fallen asleep on an arm. Upon being awakened, I found I could not move my arm, and I would have to use my other arm to get it moving and get the blood flowing. When my oldest son was little, he would often fall asleep in the strangest positions. We would be awakened in the middle of the night to loud crying because he had no feeling in his arm or in a leg. We had to reassure him that it was going to be okay. We would begin to rub the affected limb until the circulation began to flow again and he got his feeling back.

The pattern for our lives is clearly seen in the humanity of Jesus. After coming up out of the chaos of Jordan's dark waters, having submitted to being identified with us in our darkened state and immersed, heaven opened and the voice of the Father spoke the word of affirmation to His one and only Son. The Father said, "This is My beloved Son, in whom I am well-pleased" (Matt. 3:17).

The Father took pleasure and delight in the uniqueness of His only Son. In the strength of that affirming and confirming voice, Jesus yielded to the Spirit and was "driven" into the wilderness. The compelling drive of the Spirit was causing Him to enter into the sufferings of a race that had been alienated from the God who had created them. As humans we found our lives reduced to little more than a long series of performances offered in the hope of obtaining what was originally given as gift. We were starved for affirmation and were driven to perform in order to be affirmed. This was certainly a great part of Adam's nightmare.

TEMPTATION IN THE TIME OF TRANSITION

In the wilderness Jesus endured a forty-day period of transition. He entered the hallway between His life in the carpenter shop and His life as the wise master builder of His Father's house. There in the hallway He was tempted forty days and forty nights to perform in order to prove He was who the Father affirmed He was.

The tempter approached Him boldly. With every

temptation the opening line was, "If You are the Son of God..." In other words, "If You are who God says You are, then prove it." But when we come to the light as He is in the light, we know by affirmation who we truly are. And when we know who we truly are, we no longer need to prove it to anyone.

The tempter tried to get Jesus to prove His identity by doing things that would be an indication of His status and stature. "If You are the Son of God, turn these stones into bread!" The Savior's response was interesting. He said, "Man shall not live by bread alone..." (Matt. 4:4, KJV).

Jesus was fully human as well as fully divine. Interestingly, He didn't respond to the enemy's argument. Instead, He took His stand on the grounds of His humanity. What is even more marvelous is that after coming out of the wilderness, He multiplied loaves on a number of occasions without any apparent effort at all. When You are the Bread of Heaven, You have no need to turn stones into bread because You need nothing outside of Youself to affirm the essence of who You are.

When the forty-day period in the hallway was completed and the enemy had tried everything he could to seduce the Savior to abort His identity and destiny, He came out of the hallway and stepped into greatness. As the Scriptures declare, He returned to Galilee in the *power of the Spirit.*

He never forgot who He was, yet when He left the wilderness, He never donned the carpenter's apron again. He would no longer be doing what only served to shape and form Him for His greater and higher purpose and calling. Now He would go about doing good and healing all who were oppressed by the seducer who demanded performance.

WAKING UP

Jesus came so that others might be brought into total aliveness and experience that aliveness at such a level that all their sleeping parts might begin to tingle and wake up. Then they would no longer wake up in the dark night of their soul, crying out for the recovery of what was lost, stolen or destroyed by the sinister master of illusion and shadows.

The acid test for Jesus was going "home" to the hometown crowd. They couldn't let go of their perception of who He was to them before, yet they also resented that He offered His miracle-working power to other places before He offered it to them.

When the light came, they loved the darkness rather than the light, so they pressed the snooze button on their spiritual alarm clocks and slept through their visitation. They dreamed that they threw Him over the cliff on the border of their little and limited town. But since they never really saw Him in the light of who He truly was, He passed through their midst without even being noticed.

Certainly none of us want meaningful relationships to end abruptly. Yet moments and seasons come when we have passed through an exit door into a hallway where there appears to be a narrowing of our options. Some of the people we're in relationship with can't go there with us.

There in that low valley of dark shadows, we see for

ourselves where we have been and gain a fresh vision of where we are going. We become aware of the power of our choices, and we begin to choose the new identity and the new creation that is our true reality. As we begin to emerge from the hallway, we come to discover that the people we thought would celebrate our growth are actually resentful of our transformation. At the same time, there is a great and significant number of others whom we have never met who are ready to *see us* and able to *receive us* for who we really are. The outcomes are nothing less than supernatural.

What keeps you hanging on to toxic relationships?

Making

the funda-

mental shift

from doing

to being

Becoming Who You Are

To be nobody but yourself in a world
which is doing its best, day and night,
to make you like everybody else is to
fight the hardest battle which any
human being can fight...but never stop
fighting!

—E. E. CUMMINGS

IF I AM TO MOVE FORWARD WITH GOD AND EMBRACE THE
feel of destiny, I have to shed my "goatskins." Jacob
sought to trick his dying father, Isaac, into giving him
his brother Esau's blessing. He did this by covering himself with goatskins in order to feel and smell like his

brother Esau. (See Genesis 27.) In the encounter between Jacob and Isaac, Isaac said, "Come close and let me *feel you,* my son."

My pain had led me for so long that I couldn't feel as deeply as I was created to feel. I had put on so many layers of "skins" that to touch the real me required a stripping away of the less-than-human part of me. When I say "less than human," I am referring to our human tendency to resort to lower levels of living that are more akin to the beastly side of life.

Like goats, we tend to "butt" our heads into things that seem to refuse to move when we want them to move. The goatskins represent that "beastly" side of us to which we revert when our frustration level is so high that we can't manage to get to where we want to go.

MAKING THE ROUGH PLACES SMOOTH

Changing mind-sets in the hallway requires coming to the Father without "goatskins" on our hands (our works) and chests (our heart). We tried to be someone else in order to obtain what at one level we felt we would never get. We wore skins because we chose to "play it safe."

Part of the process is taking off the goatskins and entering a place of intimacy just the way we are. That takes a bit of undressing. To wear the rough skin of a goat requires that we kill the goat first. Putting on the rough skin of something that is dead creates a definite barrier to intimacy. Dead things are rough. Jacob's real texture was "smooth." He presented himself as exactly the opposite of who he truly was because he was trying to live the life of another. *That* is second-hand living.

The dead beast provided the cloak that hid Jacob from his father. It is interesting that years later the aging Jacob is handed a multicolored tunic that his sons had dipped in the blood of a goat. They slew the goat in an effort to convince their father that their brother was dead. By getting rid of Joseph, they hoped to restore their intimacy with their father. They wanted from Jacob what *he* never received from Isaac, his father.

When Joseph's brothers saw that he received what they never had, they too resorted to the cloak of death to hide their real longing and unmet need for intimacy. Somewhere in our unfinished business we chose responses that made us "rough" in order to try to obtain what we thought we could never have. However, "roughness" will never enable us to step into greatness. Those who prefer the "rough" ways of dead things over the smooth and seemingly weaker approach of their own humanness are in actual fact more like Esau. They are despising their birthright and will sell their intended greatness for "a mess of pottage" to satisfy their immediate craving. *But it is the divine intention to make the rough places smooth.* (See Luke 3:5.)

Like Jacob, we have to learn that the rough things of death never bring the smooth results of life in the flow of intended greatness. We cannot live in a manner that is reflective of greatness when we have clothed ourselves with a rough exterior of dead works. When people don't "feel" life in what we are serving them, they lose their feel for genuine intimacy with us.

We need to let go of the fear that what we were born to will never be given to us. We discover in the hallway that we have believed we'll lose out on something if we don't wear the skins. However, what God wants us to see is that when we remove the skins, we will also sluff off the barriers and roadblocks to intended greatness. The temptation to keep on the skins is based on the belief that we are better off avoiding the pain of feeling emotionally weak, rather than risking transparency for the sake of intimacy.

Somewhere on the journey to adulthood, Jacob lost his feelings in relationship to his father. His natural response of being a smooth and peaceful man brought with it rejection from his father. The Bible makes it very clear that Isaac withheld a certain amount of affection from his younger son. Jacob felt that withdrawal quite deeply. In order to avoid continued disapproval for being who he was, he denied his essential nature and buried the hurt under layers of dead skins. He didn't only disconnect from his father—*he disconnected from himself.*

Life takes on a whole new dimension when we allow our minds to be transformed. The ingrained patterning of our unconscious and unacknowledged behaviors has impeded our ability to move forward toward greatness. We have built within us a mental model of what we believe reality to be.

Distinguishing Between What We Want and What We Need

When we admit that we have covered our uniqueness with rough, dead skin, we are also at a place where we can distinguish the things we want from the things we need. What Jacob *wanted* was the birthright, but what he *needed* was to be affirmed by his father.

124

He protected himself from his need for his father's affection because he felt it could not be met. But at the same time, he drove himself to obtain what he wanted more than anything else—the right of the firstborn.

In actuality, God was going to give Jacob what was promised. That was already a settled issue. The need that Jacob had for his father's approval and affirmation was truly nonnegotiable. Isaac was too blind to see what his son needed more than anything else. The birthright and the blessing were at some level negotiable, because God was the one who promised it would be given—not Isaac. At the moment Jacob went into the tent, what he wanted (the blessing of the birthright) conflicted with what he needed (an affirmation by his father for who he truly was).

Confusing our wants with our needs gets us in trouble in the pursuit of purpose. This confusion also makes it necessary for us to experience the process that leads us through the hallway on the way toward intended greatness. Jacob wanted the birthright, which was the right of the firstborn. If we break that down to where you and I live, he wanted to be *first*.

Yet did he *need* to be first? Was Jacob any less of a person because his brother arrived first? We know that the drive to be first was in him from the womb, because when Esau emerged from the womb, his heel was in the clutches of his slightly younger brother. Hence they called him Jacob, which meant "heel catcher."

In the hallway we begin to see things in a different light. There we are invited to take an inventory of the difference between what we want and what we truly need. We soon discover for ourselves that we have mixed up what we need and what we want. It becomes apparent to us that we have done things that provided us the greatest favor and pleasure even if those things were not appropriate.

BOUND TO A FALSE IMAGE

When we don't fully know who we are and when we cannot see ourselves in the light of the truth, we remain bound to a false image. Idolatry is believing that someone else's life is more worthy than ours. When that occurs, we adopt their behaviors in order to get their results.

Walter Brueggemann, the Presbyterian theologian says, "Idolatry is second-hand living." Jacob made a choice to believe that if he were to get what he wanted from his father, he had to live his brother's life. So he went into the tent of blessing thinly disguised as his brother. Wearing the skins of "I'll do whatever I have to do to get what I want the most" provides us the exact opposite of what we need.[1]

The things I do are vitally connected to my perception of who I am. I am building my reality (true or false) by everything I choose to believe is true—even if it is false. I am influencing my future, either consciously or unconsciously, by the choices I am making. Every choice brings with it another possibility. Every choice affects every outcome.

My definition of reality determines the choices I make. If I live in an illusion or mask reality, I am shaping my future. Similarly, I am also shaping my future if I am living in the truth and embracing reality.

Although I can (and do) give credence to God's sovereignty, that doesn't excuse me from the results of my actions. Instead, He requires that I take total responsibility for what I think, feel, say and do. The sovereign God does not accept excuses for our choices—particularly when the results are the opposite of what He intended.

He invites us to continually get feedback so that we can learn how to make the course corrections we need to get to our intended destination. The apostle Paul said it this way: "Do not be deceived, God is not mocked, for whatever someone sows, so also do they reap" (Gal. 6:7). That feedback process is important in learning how to take His lead and follow Him into our intended destiny.

BREAKTHROUGH

One day I received a phone call from my father. The crisis I had gone through had awakened some feelings in him, and he needed to talk. This was unusual for Dad.

Dad didn't find it easy to open up and share. Self-disclosure was not one of his strong suits, and it wasn't one of mine, either. Put the two of us together, and our conversations were usually short, to the point and unemotional—unless we were disagreeing about something (which was a common occurrence).

Dad told me that he needed to talk. I heard in his voice a sense of disturbance. I responded that he needed to tell me what was going on. He said, "I can't talk about it over the phone. When can I come and see you?" I was about to say, "Give me a few hours," but before I could get the words out he said, "I am coming over right now!"

Dad arrived about twenty minutes later. I was downstairs in the study. He looked deeply troubled, and I was aware that he was dealing with intense emotional pain. As I have already mentioned, Dad and I have had our challenges. But through it all there has always been a deep bond and connection between us. I have come to realize that we both knew what the other was feeling without having to say a whole lot about it. Yet never processing those feelings with each other kept us back from a great deal of wholeness that we could have given to each other over the years.

TERRORS IN THE NIGHT

For six months prior to the exposure of my betrayal, I was awakened every night at 3 A.M. sharp. This took place without the aid of an alarm clock. There was a great deal of tension and stress rising up. Things were brought to the light, and I lived in a state of anxiety and dread about the future. I had no tangible evidence to "prove" that something wasn't quite right, yet in my gut I was disturbed. In one of his letters Paul wrote, "I had no rest for my spirit" (2 Cor. 2:13). I kept referring to that verse many times in prayer. I also confided in my wife and my leadership team (which included my betrayer). I was not aware of the dynamics of the seeds of destruction that had been sown against me. I just could "feel" the unrest, and I had a sense of uncertainty and fear all around me.

When I awoke each night at 3 A.M., I saw a dark figure with two red eyes, draped from head to toe in a black cowl or hooded cape, facing me in the night at the edge of the bed.

I had previously experienced strange dreams from time to time during times of transition in my life. On two or three occasions I have had "terrors in the night" where we think we are awake when in fact we are asleep. The terror is so great that we can't escape. Somehow our mind alerts us to the fact that we are indeed asleep, and we fight to wake up. It seems to take forever for our body to respond to our will to wake up. Once we do wake up, we shake ourself, perhaps turn the light on, get a glass of water and say, "Thank God that's over."

In this vision, however, the red eyes peered icy cold at me through the cowl, penetrating my soul with intimidation.

I was used to spiritual warfare, and I had a degree of success in setting people free from the snares of the adversary. Deliverance from demonic power is part of our birthright. Our authority in the unseen realm includes authority over *all* the powers of the enemy. While at that season I was aware of dealing with some tough things in my own life, I had long ago learned how to deal with the forces of darkness sent to harass me.

As foreboding as this vision was, I could not discern the message behind it. The vision returned like clockwork every night for six months.

Later I found out just how diabolical things were that were taking place within the context of the friend who betrayed me. There are always reasons that the powers of darkness find access and the legal right to harass the people of God. We need to recognize where those places are and set up watches against such devices. Remember, in my own heart—in my blind spot—there were things that I couldn't even see, let alone check.

This ominous warning recurred because there was someone in my life who was driven by malice toward me. Over the months I continued to pray about these warnings, because I wanted clarity from God about what I was wrestling with and my reasons for feeling discomfort. When everything came out into the open, it all made sense, and the nightly warnings came to an end.

LONGING FOR FATHER

What I was about to learn there in the family room, standing face to face with my dad, was that he was also being awakened every night (at about three in the morning)—but not by an evil principality. He was awakened by a deep longing for his father. My dad was crying out for his father.

My grandfather died in the late 1960s of a heart attack on a cold and snowy winter night. The weather in New York that winter was a record breaker. Dad's business was on the north shore of Staten Island, and we lived on the south shore. It was at least a thirty-minute drive from the house to the office. Mom was the bookkeeper, and she had to make sure that I got off to school. She would drive to work about two hours after Dad left each morning.

But whenever the weather was inclement, my grandfather would take her to the office because he didn't want her to drive in bad weather. This involved driving from his house on the north shore all the way to the south shore. It was quite a hike—fighting traffic the whole way.

Late one Sunday night in January of 1967, the snow began to pile up—not by the inch, but by the foot. Grandpa got up from his bed, put on his coat and went out to shovel the driveway and clean off his car so that he could pick up my mom in the morning. He didn't tell Grandma what he was doing. He just saw the heavy snow and felt he needed to clean off the car and the driveway.

It was far too much of a load for him to handle in the cold that late at night. When he finished, he came back inside and smoked a cigarette. He then went back to bed and a little while later got up to go to the bathroom.

Grandma was startled as she heard a loud thud. She sprang up and ran into the bathroom, only to find Grandpa on the floor, having hit his head on the porcelain tub on the way down. He was already gone, yet one of his hands was clutching his chest. He had suffered a fatal heart attack. Grandpa had a hole in his heart and had been under a doctor's care for years. The combination of the strain of shoveling snow in the cold, the condition in his heart and the cigarette all compounded the situation. Grandpa was gone.

Dad was devastated. I will never forget those memories. I was ten years old when Grandpa died. Dad spent months grieving his loss. There would be nights that Dad wouldn't come home until late at night. He wouldn't tell Mom and me where he was, and we would worry. We later found out he spent hours at the grave site, grieving the loss of his father.

There were times that he would lock himself in the bathroom, and I would hear him cry for long periods of time. As a child I felt so helpless. I needed to do something, but I didn't know what. It was also around this time that Dad began to be more erratic in his responses at home. His anger would get the best of him.

I didn't understand the path he was heading down until years later. When I got to college, I learned about the stages of grief and began to understand how human beings process loss. Dad didn't have anyone with whom he felt he could process his grief, so he processed it alone. I am not even sure he allowed God to help him sort it out, because he was already hiding from Him because of the self-blame and guilt he felt over his brother's death.

All of that began to come back to my memory while Dad stood in the family room, wanting to sort out all his feelings. He missed his father. He opened up and shared that he knew his dad loved him, but he so wanted to hear those words from his father. Here we were—a father and a son *both* coming to grips with our longing for affirmation, standing face to face, wanting from each other what we felt we had not been given ourselves. In a powerful and tender moment of embrace, I was able to let Dad know just how much I needed his love and how much I loved him. I shared some deeply personal feelings and affirmed him in those areas where he had been a significant figure in my own overall development. We had stripped off the skins and laid bare our hearts.

He asked me to pray for him, and there in that

moment, I found myself crying out to God the Father to provide for my dad what he felt he needed but never received from his own father. There are some who believe that a moment in time comes in which the parent-child relationship roles are reversed. I do not believe that at all.

From my perspective, as spiritual and superior as it sounds for the roles to change, I think it is a form of dishonor and a lack of respect. Dad will always be my father, and I will always be his son. I cannot become his dad, and I would never try to be that to him. He will always have his dad for a father, and there will always be in him that longing to know not only that his father loved him, but also to find out who he was by having his father connect with him beyond the role of provider.

He was crying out for his father to be present with him in his own pain, for someone strong to help him process his pain and tell him how to survive and move on. Dad was troubled because he was now the same age as his father when he died. As he sorted through his own mortality, he was longing for that relationship again because he needed his dad more than ever. He was touching his feeling of being alone and cut off from his dad.

HONORING FATHER AND MOTHER

Healing prayer that brings us into the presence of the Father can transport us from the pain of absence to the joy of presence. Honoring fathers and mothers isn't about ignoring their unfinished business, much less denying their behaviors if they happened to be abusive.

Some individuals who were abused feel guilty because

they have strong feelings of animosity toward their parents. They wrestle with guilt because the Scriptures declare in Ephesians 6:2, "Honor your father and mother (which is the first commandment with a promise), that it may be well with you, and that you may live long on the earth."

The apostle Paul plainly declared that in honoring our parents it will be well with us and we will have longevity. I am grateful for the parents I have been given. While we had our skirmishes and challenges, I am deeply grateful that our family was never torn and fragmented. Of course, this doesn't mean that we had it all together. Like everyone else, we had our dysfunction.

Paying attention to the way our parents shaped our lives and our identities can be healing. It will enable us to sort out our past and move forward toward maturity. In an atmosphere of safety and acceptance, we can come to a place in our growth where we are able to celebrate our lives together and nurture each other.

Those who come from single-parent homes or who had primary caregivers who were not their parents can still apply the truth of this. We all need to know the love and acceptance that is ours in Christ, and we need to apply it to the untouched, unhealed and unaffirmed areas of our lives. When we make room for the Father to bring us through the low places in our lives, we need to realize that there are others waiting to bring us into His healing presence. For it is in His presence that our lives can be put back together again on a whole new foundation.

In the low places, or valleys of our lives, our preferences are discarded, and our sense of well-being begins to rise and be built up. Sometimes before we get to that low place, a great deal of our activity may be from an ego-driven need to *prove* and *perform* our way to acceptance and recognition. When we learn the difference between false image and true image, between needs-driven principles and behaviors, we will be on our way through the hallway toward the door that is just ahead of us—the door to greatness.

Are you imitating the life of another or truly living your own?

Dipping

into destiny—

finding won-

derful gifts

that were

unsought

Dipping Into Destiny

Like many of the finest things in life, like happiness, tranquility and fame, the gain that was most precious was not the thing sought, but one that came of itself in the search for something else.
—Justice Benjamin N. Cardozo

In 1754 Sir Horace Walpole, an Englishman, coined the word *serendipity* in a letter to Horace Mann. Walpole was an earl of Oxford, a member of Parliament and a graduate of Eton College. Mann was serving in Florence, Italy, at the time as an envoy. They were close personal friends.

Walpole had a flare and penchant for writing letters. Many of them are still available at certain large libraries in England and America.[1]

Walpole was also an avid reader and had enjoyed an ancient Persian fairytale called "The Three Princes of Serendipity." Serendipity was the ancient name for the island known today as Ceylon. These three princes, the sons of a king, had adventurous spirits and traveled the world. Yet, no matter what their intent, when they went out looking for one thing, other unexpected things happened. These meaningful coincidences gave them valuable insights they hadn't sought.

In his letter to Horace Mann, Walpole was commenting on the story as it related to life itself. He coined the word *serendipity* to describe this phenomenon: "Because as their highnesses traveled they were always making discoveries by accident or sagacity of things they were not in quest of." The phrase he coined began to be used by Mann, then those with whom they conversed, until it found its way into the dictionary.

Serendipity is defined as "the ability of finding valuable things unexpectedly and not sought for." It deals with making desirable yet unsought-for discoveries by accident. Walpole's approach to the term *serendipity* was tied to his feeling that when we "dip into life with a serene mind-set and surrender to what life serves us," we will experience favorable outcomes in places where we did not look. Of course, behind life is the unseen hand of God, ordering all things after the counsel of His will.

For example, a man was once trying to find a way to keep wine from turning sour. Instead, he accidentally found a way to kill the bacteria that can destroy life. He named what he discovered in that serendipitous event *pasteurization*. I guess by now you realize his notable name was Louis Pasteur.

The threat of smallpox created another moment of serendipity. A man named Jenner found that a memory stored in his mind suddenly "popped up." The memory had been lying dormant for years, actually since he was young and in love. While dating a young milkmaid in his early teens, she informed Edward Jenner that it would be impossible for her to contract smallpox, since as a child she had contracted cowpox.

Years later there was a severe threat of smallpox in his nation, and it was rapidly reaching epidemic proportions. In a flash of insight, out of his memory from years before came the words from this young woman, which he used to create the vaccine for smallpox. This vaccine literally saved the lives of multiplied thousands in his day—and who can count how many since then? That is a classic example of serendipity.

SAUL'S SERENDIPITY

There was a day when a young man was awakened to find that his father's two donkeys had wandered out of the gate and into the wilderness. These two donkeys were valuable to the young man's father, so at the request of his father, he obediently went out with one of his father's servants in search of the donkeys. After he spent three days searching without results, he was ready to quit and go home.

But the servant knew the territory more intimately

than the young man did. He helped the young man appreciate what was available to him in the place where they were. You see, the young man had no idea where he was standing.

He was standing within the borders of the territory of a well-known man who could "see" into the invisible and had insight into the meaning behind life's adventures. There was a *seer* in the region. God blessed this seer with powerful prophetic insight and awareness. The hired hand offered to lead the young man into the presence of the man of God.

The young man knew how important it was to honor a servant of the Lord. But he had already spent all his resources trying to find the donkeys. He couldn't "afford" to take the next step and connect with someone who could see what he could not. The servant, however, had a great deal of silver in his possession. It was more than enough to honor the man of God with a gift.

Little did the young man know it at the time, but while he was out looking for the donkeys, God had already shown the seer that this young man was on a journey. The entire purpose of the loss of the donkeys and the quest of an obedient son was to lead the young man on a "wild-donkey chase" to a place he never would have gone on his own. He met a man he never expected to meet, and he found that God had set the entire thing up to give the young man a throne he didn't believe he deserved. The story of young Saul is filled with what Walpole called "serendipity," for he came upon something quite valuable while he was looking for something else.

Notice that the servant appointed by his father said

very little until the moment of crisis. When the young Saul was lost, out of money and ready to quit, the servant had the know-how and resources to go forward.

It didn't cost Saul a thing, because whatever belonged to the servant was actually given to him by Saul's father. So the servant held these resources in trust for Saul until the appropriate time.

Samuel had already been informed by God that a young man from the territory of Benjamin was on his way and in need of help. When we enter the hallway, we are at a place where things begin to happen to us that we aren't looking for. As I have already stated, life is a series of connected and related things. We don't know how our lost donkeys connect to our intended greatness—but they can be the means for getting us out of the hallway and into the doorway of destiny. God knows what it will take to move us forward on a journey that we could not have planned for ourselves.

LOSING TO GAIN

God has arranged it so that there are certain things He allows us to "lose" in the hallway. They are things that we once had a grasp of but don't any longer. He creates an event that moves us toward chasing what we lost, and then He brings us to a point where we have looked every place we know how to look. Then, at the point where we want to turn around and go back, we hit the "point of no return" (PNR).

At that moment, if we will ask for our missing piece, we will discover that there is a "Servant" (if you please), One called alongside to help who is standing by us every step of the way. This Special Helper has come because of the sacrifice of Another. It is because of the finished, "paid-in-full" work of the Master that the Holy Spirit has been sent to accompany us on the journey. He has been sent to us as the "earnest" of our inheritance. He is the One who assures us that all will be well.

The servant produced silver for the gift that Saul needed to offer to the seer. Silver symbolizes redemption and the power to buy back what has been lost to us. In and of ourselves, we can't afford to buy back the inheritance and destiny we have lost. Someone else has already paid the price for us. He gives us what we need as a gift so that we in turn can give it as a gift to someone else.

In the hallway we begin to realize that we can't afford to buy our own way into greatness. Freely we have received, and freely we can then give. This is grace with no strings attached. When we are given what we didn't earn, we can then give it away to others without any expectation of return, since it was never something we worked for anyway.

ENABLED TO EMBRACE THE FUTURE

The hired hand said nothing until Saul hit rock bottom. It is there at that precise moment of the PNR that a gift of grace will be presented to us. This gift of grace will enable us to take the next necessary step toward greatness. If you ask me, that was the point where Saul was invited by God to dip into *destiny*.

At the point of total frustration with his lack of ability to recover what he had lost, Saul was provided with the crucial "missing piece" by the servant. The "quarter of a shekel of silver" was quite a significant sum. It created the kind of tranquility that enabled Saul to make a fundamental shift in his thinking and to surrender to the serendipity God had for him. There at that moment he was enabled to embrace the future with hope and trust that the outcome would be exceedingly, abundantly above all that he could ask, think or even imagine.

God is always at least a step ahead of us in the hallway. Twenty-four hours before Saul hit the point of no return, God told Samuel he was on the way. Samuel had been asking God for a king. Saul had been asking God for the recovery of his father's donkeys. Neither Saul nor Samuel was looking for each other to begin with. Each was looking for what was necessary to satisfy the dominant need of the moment.

Saul was feeling the weight of having to recover what was precious to his father. Even though Saul and Samuel didn't realize it at first, they were both looking for each other. It merely took an event in the hallway to create the encounter.

As an insert, despite Saul ultimately allowing his insecurity to destroy the greatness God had intended for him, he *was* God's choice. Things were clearly moving along in his favor and in a flow. He could have become the very antithesis of what he ended up becoming—had he recognized God's love in the journey on which he found himself. Saul allowed his own unfinished business to prevent him from truly stepping into greatness. On the outside he was a king, but he remained a slave to his own fears on the inside. He never learned at a deep level how to travel light.

In any event, there at the point of no return abundant

resources were available to bring him to a place where he could never bring himself. God was about to offer him a future that he was not even aware he was looking for. When Saul and the servant finally arrived in the region where Samuel lived, they were on a God-ordained "collision course" with the future.

They met at the gate of the city. At that place of access and egress, as one was coming in and the other was going out, there was an immediate awareness on the part of Samuel that this was the man of whom God spoke twenty-four hours earlier. At the moment of their meeting, Saul did not know whom he was questioning. He asks, "Is the seer here?" At the moment he asks the question, he also faces the very one whom he is seeking.

DIRECTING THROUGH INDIRECTION

This story is the story of our lives once we find our-selves in the hallway and surrender to a process that goes beyond the limits of our understanding. We can't lean on our own understanding if we expect to be led by the Spirit. The Spirit does not lead us through a formula or by a set of dyed-in-the-wool, clear-cut rules.

It is a dance. The more we become acquainted with the leading of God, the more we will learn that His direction comes by *indirection*. He is the Unseen Hand behind what Walpole referred to as *serendipity*. God *is* the author of meaningful coincidence. It is not some "chance occurrence"—though unenlightened humanity may call it that. Remember that "chance" is merely God's pen name when He wants to keep us in the posture of trust and wonder (which I believe is most of the time).

Saul was looking for donkeys, not for a throne—or was he?

When we are in *the flow of God's serendipity,* there comes to the surface many of the things that have been hidden in our hearts in that "unknown" place, *things that we never allowed ourselves to believe were possible.*

If he had the donkeys in his heart, then why did Samuel, after introducing himself to Saul, say, "Stay with me today and tomorrow I will tell you all that is on your *heart.*" Immediately Samuel goes on to say, "As for the donkeys which were lost, they have been found." (See 1 Samuel 9:19–20.) At a cursory glance, we might ignore those two statements and never make the connection between head and heart. But then we would miss the doorway that is standing just ahead of us. In view at the end of the hallway there is hanging an invitation: "Step Into Greatness."

What preoccupies your mind that is keeping you from honoring what is on your heart?

SECTION THREE

GREATNESS: THE DESTINY

THAT AWAITS YOU

The
moment
you see
what freedom
truly is

Uncovering Your Uniqueness

> Remember that you are unique. If that
> is not fulfilled, then something won-
> derful has been lost.
> —MARTHA GRAHAM

A FEW YEARS AGO I WAS IN A LARGE THIRD WORLD
country for a series of meetings that lasted for over a
month. It was a wonderful experience. Staying in that
nation for an extended period of time gave me an
opportunity to study the culture and see how the people
of that country embraced life.

I saw abject poverty and unimagined opulence side

by side on the streets. I also saw the incredible resilience of character that was in the people. Somehow I had grace to see them through "new eyes." I was delighted to have been given the opportunity to connect with people I never knew who lived literally halfway around the globe.

At our core we are all made from the same clay. We all have a need to love and to be loved, and we all long to make a difference. We want our word in the sentence of life to be meaningful and to leave a legacy behind for others to appreciate, enjoy and hopefully to grow on. That deeper, more passionate yearning for legacy awaits our readiness. It is the passion for our greatness in God.

These dear people had such incredible personalities and giftings that my wife and I just fell in love with them. However, something troubled me the more I observed it. We went all around that nation and stayed in plenty of hotels. Each hotel we stayed in had a television in each room. No matter where we went in the nation, much of what we saw on television was a "copied" version of an American talk show, music show, game show or something similar. The titles were only slightly changed, and the programs had the same formats and the same kinds of clothes as the American counterparts they were emulating. On these television shows they did everything, *and I mean everything*, the way we do it in America.

At one level, emulating the American culture can be quite flattering. On another level, when all you are doing is "copying" something or someone else, there is a deeper and more vital issue at stake. It takes a certain amount of ingenuity to replicate someone else's style and creation. *However, we can lose our own sense of creativity in the process.* These incredibly gifted people were plenty creative in their own right. Yet when it came to media, they apparently believed that their creativity was not sufficient to attract the attention of their own constituency. Someone else had a "better way" than they did.

We don't always realize what we are doing when we are devaluing whom God made us uniquely to be. It happens in subtle ways, and unfortunately some individuals never break out of the copy mode of borrowing what belongs to someone else instead of finding what belongs to them alone.

Christ in *you* (the hope of fulfilling all of God's intention for your life) will be intrinsically different from Christ in others. Not that He is different, for He never changes—but rather that He has made each one of us unique. His power alone gives that uniqueness full expression.

In my opinion, one of the reasons we resort to copying someone or something else is that we don't believe it is possible to have in life what we really desire. We're not convinced that there really is a place that has been prepared *for us.* We have yet to fully affirm all the attributes of the "new man." So the residue memory from former patterns and symbols in our awareness of the "old man" hinder us from becoming all we were meant to be.

THE LIFE OF COMPARISON AND COMPETITION

Buried under the layers of misperceptions, misconceptions and unfinished business lies a hidden treasure. Most of us don't even know it is there, although it calls to us from within by the Spirit in ways we have not fully discerned.

A landmark work on the issue of false assumptions regarding the continued existence of two natures in us (the old man and the new man) is Richard C. Needham's classic work, *Birthright: Christian, Do You Know Who You Are?* Needham successfully and masterfully argues from the words of Jesus and Paul that there is no longer an old man inside us by nature.[1]

Nevertheless, our real challenge is that we have a *memory* of our old nature. The old messages, scripts and deep patterns of a false and world-shaped self-image can at times "pop up" out of nowhere to cause us to behave in ways that seem totally opposite of who we truly are and desire to be. It is difficult in a world that values the superficial projection of a false image to find a way to discover, uncover and celebrate our uniqueness.

Since we all have areas where we want to improve, we tend to dismiss and devalue our strengths and focus on what we don't have. If someone else happens to have something that we do not seem to possess, we often forget that we also have certain strengths that they were not given. Adam did so in the Garden when he focused on the one tree that would take him out of the flow of God's pleasure while standing in the midst of so many other trees from which he could have freely chosen to eat.

The tree of the knowledge of good and evil becomes

in our experience a place where we exhibit less than life-affirming behaviors. When I believe you have something that I need, I may start acting in ways to either obtain it or to take it from you.

Comparison is the twin sister of competition. Once we begin comparing ourselves with one another, we are only a few steps away from competing with each other. Competition can lead to a wide variety of unbecoming behaviors such as criticism, sarcasm, gossip, minimizing (cutting people down to a size that we find suitable) and de-legitimizing—to name but a few.

When we *release* the need to compare, we *increase* the opportunity to create. Creative ability inherent within our spirits, never affirmed and never discovered, lies dormant until the appointed time comes for us to let go of our need to be like everyone else. At that point we become true to our God-given identity.

When we find those swings in our words and actions between whom we used to be and whom we want to be, we can easily doubt that we really have a new identity. We have learned to practice behaviors that enable us to get by and survive in a world where uniqueness is rarely affirmed.

I began to let go of a number of learned behaviors when I was on my way through the hallway. During my devotional time I found that words like *authentic* and *genuine* began to come to me in prayer. The Father was asking me to discover how to be authentic and true to the core values He placed within me. Having spent so much time unaware of my constant striving to please everyone, I hit a point where I no longer wanted to do that anymore. I was tired of performing. I was tired of living up to everyone else's expectations. The moment of truth came as an epiphany that seems somewhat humorous to me now—but when it happened, it was anything other than humorous.

RESISTING—AND INSISTING

I needed to get away for a while. When we were mopping up after my crisis had taken place, there came a moment that I just couldn't bear to hear any more of the horror stories we were uncovering.

I had registered months before for a conference in the Midwest, but I found myself "too busy" to break away and attend. I had already paid a large registration fee, but I was willing to forgo the money. It was a week-long event. Each day had eight hours of sessions. The seminar was designed to help us understand ourselves, our motivations and how those things applied to our careers. It was the kind of event that businesses send their employees to when they want to enhance their job performance. Since I had no desire to sit in intense training sessions for eight hours a day, I decided to cancel the trip. I knew the information would be valuable, but what I really wanted was just to get away and vegetate.

I called the registrar and politely thanked her for the opportunity to attend this "invitation only" seminar, but I explained that I would have to come another time. Her response was exactly what I expected.

She began to question my reason for canceling after having already paid in full for the event. I responded that I was busy with too many other things (which was an excuse). Apparently she read through my excuse and continued to ask me questions. What caught me off guard were the questions she asked.

When I had filled out the registration form for this conference, I answered a number of routine questions, including my age, occupation, marital status and educational background. With my registration form in front of her she said, "Oh, I see you are a minister, is that correct?"

I replied, "Yes, I am."

"Well then," she said, "have you prayed and asked God by His Holy Spirit whether or not you are supposed to cancel your time with us?"

I was taken back. Then I was angry, and in my head I was thinking things like, *Who does this lady think she is, asking about my prayer life and my walk with God?* When I didn't respond immediately, and after a long "uh" from me, she asked, "You do pray and ask God for His wisdom and guidance in all that you do as a minister, don't you?"

"Of course!" I retorted with a what-nerve-you-have attitude in my voice, which she heard louder than the words "of course."

"Well then," she said, "it would seem to me that if God wanted you to be at this conference, He would be able to tell you whether or not your decision not to attend was pleasing to Him."

I was furious.

She didn't even give me a chance to breathe. "I will call you back in an hour after you have prayed—*then* you can give me your answer."

She was not at all impolite. In fact, she was quite gracious—even in her questioning and posturing with me.

But I was indignant: *Who is this lady, whom I don't even know, that she would presume to tell me that I need to pray about a decision to attend this stupid conference?* Suffice it to say, my attitude was anything other than receptive toward her.

An hour later the phone rang, and I wasn't surprised when she was on the line.

She wasn't surprised either when I said that I hadn't prayed.

She didn't miss a beat. "I'll call back in another hour."

I couldn't believe this lady. *Who did she think she was?* I didn't like being bullied into a corner with the demand that I do something. She was pressing all the wrong buttons, and as far as I was concerned, she didn't know with whom she was tangling.

Actually, the reverse was true—I didn't know with whom *I* was tangling. God was meddling with me through this unknown servant of His, and I was quite disturbed that He didn't even ask my permission! I have to let you know that I was even more determined *not* to pray the second time she asked me to!

By the time the next phone call came, I had already canceled my airline reservations. I wasn't going— *absolutely, positively not.* The canceled plane reservations didn't intimidate this lady in the least. She then proceeded to offer to connect me with her travel agent and rebook a ticket. I assured her that I had no other options because all the available flights had already left. The earliest I could arrive would be late morning, but this was not permitted because the first three hours were orientation, and we signed an agreement when we registered that if we didn't show up for orientation we would forfeit the right to attend the conference.

Years ago I discerned the principle that whenever I was about to experience a level of breakthrough in the Spirit, I would encounter incredible resistance. The more powerful the truth, the greater the resistance to the truth from forces within and without. This time it wasn't the powers of darkness—it was me! Intuitively there was an awareness inside me that what was really going on was that I didn't want to face something that needed to be dealt with! As it says in Proverbs, "The heart knows its own bitterness" (Prov. 14:10).

I was quite disturbed at the persistence of this stranger who was meddling with my life. It was now late in the evening, and the event began at 8 A.M. the following morning. It was *impossible* to get there, and I didn't want to go.

She said one final time, "I will give you one more hour to pray about this, and then whatever you decide will be fine." At that point she told me good-bye and hung up the phone.

I went into the other room where my wife was sitting on the sofa watching television and sat down next to her. She had not been privy to my phone conversations during the last three hours, although she did hear me say something earlier about deciding not to attend the seminar. When I sat down, she saw that I was disturbed and asked me why I was troubled.

I explained that I had called the registrar to inform her company that I would not be attending the seminar. I was just about to go into a long diatribe on how upset I was at the way this lady on the other end of the phone was meddling where she didn't belong when *my wife* asked me why I was canceling the event.

I told her I was tired and that I needed just to take time to relax. There was "too much going on right now" for me to spend a week out of town for eight solid hours daily of sessions on time management and presentation skills. At that point she reminded me how much I had invested already and how I had planned to attend this conference for months.

"If you don't do it now, when will there be a more convenient time? After all, you're *always* busy!" she said.

This wasn't the response I was looking for. However, I knew that she meant well. She just wanted me to evaluate whether or not the decision I made to cancel was a wise one.

Just as I began to explain myself, she asked, "Have you *prayed* about this?" *Now* I was fit to be tied. First this stranger, then my wife—both were meddling with my prayer life.

I quickly retorted, "What does *prayer* have to do with all this?"

She said, "You felt as though this was a vital conference when you were invited to attend, and you believed that God wanted to invest in you through this event. You committed to it based on a sense of His direction!" She then went on to say, "Now that you are canceling, and it's OK if you do, are you saying that God wasn't in it to begin with?" I was ready to react when she finished by saying, "I just want you to be sure you are not missing God in all this!"

Troubled and mumbling something under my breath, I left the couch and proceeded up the stairs to grumble all by myself in the bedroom. *Who needed to pray about canceling an event I didn't have time for? Why do we have to make such a big deal about this?* As I arrived at the doorway to my bedroom and began to unpack the suitcase that I no longer needed, I let God know how disturbed I was over the situation.

As I began to "dump" all of my frustrations at the throne of grace, I felt something in my spirit get "checked" when I went to unpack my bags. It was hard to unpack in the face of the conviction of the Holy Spirit. I knew somewhere in my "knower" what was going on, and I didn't want to talk to God about it. I stopped praying and walked into the closet to rearrange my shirts just to preoccupy myself from facing this challenge to pray about something I saw as a non-prayer issue.

The lady was going to call back in forty minutes. I had to come up with one final firm excuse that would make this a settled issue. While rearranging my shirts, a thought came to me that sounded something like this, *Why wouldn't you include God in a decision to cancel an event in which you thought He was leading you to participate in the first place?*

I didn't like that question!

Then the next thought was even more direct, *Why isn't this important enough to pray about, or do you want to exclude God from your decision-making process?* I didn't like that question any better. And who was raising all of these questions anyway?

In a matter of moments I decided to pray. As I opened

my mouth to pray, another thought popped onto the viewing screen of my mind: *You don't need to pray about this; you already know this is a divine appointment for you!*

I was now upset with the strange lady I didn't know, upset with my wife whom I did know and upset at God who allowed them to know intuitively what it was I refused to admit that I knew!

The real reason I didn't want to go to this seminar was because it would challenge me to change at another level in terms of my leadership and communication styles. It was too much hard work at that moment for me to want to absorb a bunch of new material. I needed a break, and this was not a convenient time to implement new strategies anyway. I needed space and time for other things—or at least that was my reasoning.

I learned a long time ago, however, that my arms are definitely too short to box with God. I proceeded to call two friends and offered to pay them to drive me through the night to get to this conference by 8 A.M. the next morning. I was "praying" they would not be available at such short notice. But both of them were still awake, alert and had nothing pressing on their schedule. They gladly agreed to help me get to where I was going. I wanted an excuse so badly, but God chose to work things out so well that I had no more excuses.

By the time the strange lady called back and asked me, "Did you pray?" I could almost see the snicker on her lips through the phone when I said yes and that I was on the way. All she said then was to remind me to be there at eight o'clock sharp in the morning in the hotel conference room.

DIVINE SET-UPS

I hardly slept at all in the back of the van that night as Roy and Carlton drove me to the conference. We arrived at the hotel at 7:30 A.M., which gave me just enough time to take a shower and head to the conference room.

When I got to the conference room, there was a woman waiting to meet all the registrants. I just knew this was the lady who had hounded me into coming. She was sweet enough when I met her. She was kind and polite, but I still was not happy. We were handed all our conference materials while we waited for the conference host to arrive.

In the materials was a list of notables who in some way were involved with this consulting and training company over the years. They included high-profile coaches and Fortune 500 executives with national and international reputations. The list was certainly impressive to me. I had always enjoyed values-based motivational material that provided keys to being an effective leader and building a strong organization.

I made a decision that since I was there I was going to get my money's worth.

The conference host walked in the room, and I wasn't impressed at all. He was really laid back and dressed in earth-tone colors that made him look washed out. What kind of a conference host and leadership trainer doesn't know anything about appearance in the world of leadership? Certainly Steven Covey, Warren Bennis, Pat Riley or Zig Ziglar would have worn a dark suit with a power tie! Hush Puppies and Dockers weren't my "picture" of a powerful presenter or host.

I didn't know that I was about to get on the Cyclone at Coney Island and go for the ride of my life. I was about to have everything I ever thought about leadership and management challenged to the max!

I had all that great training theologically, but in terms of leadership skills I "piece-mealed" my way through the years, borrowing things from here and there. I "winged it." And I thought I was doing quite well until my refining crisis brought me face to face with my blind spot. Before I arrived at this seminar, I knew I had at least one blind spot. I thought I knew how to deal with it. I had even talked about it quite a bit with my leadership team over the past several months. I didn't know I was about to understand clearly *why* my blind spot was so devastating for me.

After the initial greetings, it was time for orientation. The seminar manual was huge, and I couldn't wait to dive into the material. I love information—the more information I have, the more I like it. I went to open the manual, and the host caught me out of the corner of his eye and basically ordered me to close the book. Orientation was first.

I was ruffled and felt as if I were back in high school being given an SAT exam by a proctor who was watching to make sure we were not opening any section of the test before we got the go-ahead to begin. Nevertheless, I followed his instructions. I focused on the host while my hands continued to clutch the notebook I had paid for but wasn't allowed to look at.

The host began to talk about our drive to gather information and the danger of having so much theory without practical application. I understood the principle well—in fact, I taught it myself. I knew he wasn't referring to me at that point. I was already past all that. Of course, I still wanted to dig into the manual!

He then began to ask us what we thought were the reasons behind the challenges and breakdown in our society, both corporately and socially. By the time he went around the room we had listed about ten or more reasons. It was an insightful exchange, and we began to interact with one another at more than a surface level.

One of the gentlemen attending was a music director at a large denominational church in the Midwest. He was a skilled organist and choral conductor, and we had a lot in common in our musical training and our taste in choral music. One of the other gentlemen attending was working in a corporate environment on the East Coast. He was looking for some way to improve his performance skills in order to advance his career. As he was sharing about his occupation, he began to bemoan all the seminars he had been to and how they had been no help to him.

The more he talked, the more time he was wasting. I wanted to jump into the information I had paid for, and this guy was taking up valuable time strolling down memory lane. The host didn't seem to mind—he just let the man talk. All the while I was counting how much it was costing of my registration dollars while this person was complaining.

Being in the "people-helping" business, it is easy to move into the "people-fixing" mode. But we can't "fix" anyone—not that it stops us from trying. After about what seemed to be thirty minutes (*thirty minutes!*) of hearing his personal frustrations rehashed over and over again, I had about as much I could stand. "People-helper" that I believed I was, I jumped right into the conversation to tie this up.

Within about thirty seconds after I offered my input, the conference host made a very polite comment that felt like a wasp sting when he finished. He said something to this effect: "While you may be able to do some counseling in your own occupational sphere, in this conference you are an attendee. I am going to ask you to refrain from offering your input since you have *no idea* where we're going!"

Now I was *convinced* I should have stayed home!

It was strange to me that he let this person keep right on talking. I was trained that in a counseling session after twenty minutes you had heard it all. After that things would begin to be repeated. I was operating on the twenty-minute paradigm—his time was definitely up, and I had another appointment!

Strange how professional and out of touch we can become in the context of "doing" what we have been taught to "do." We never learn how to be aware of what is taking place in the moment. We spend so much time passing judgment on our reality that we never fully experience all that is taking place in it. Who said this was a counseling session anyway? *Just me!*

I was a bundle of energy—much of it nervous energy—from that moment on. It had been seething below the surface all night long. But I was just becoming aware of how uncomfortable I was feeling in this situation. I was out of my preferred element. I was on someone else's turf. I was not in "control." This is another issue God deals with in the hallway. Often we exhibit unconscious control methods when fear is a motivating factor in our lives.

What made matters worse from my perspective was the fact that I knew in my heart that God was trying to tell me something. If only He would just make it plain so we could get on with the program. Of course, I thought I knew what the program of my life was. But I had been so programmed that my behaviors had become rote and routine. Yet in my heart I was crying out for change and transformation—and it seemed so far away.

The corporate guy ended up talking for two hours. By the end I was convinced I could write the guy's biography—not that I would want to. I fidgeted in my seat and tried to *appear* cool and calm. I look back now and chuckle over it all. I was like a cartoon character.

What was really uncomfortable was that the guy began to cry about his life. "This is a professional business seminar, and this guy is *crying*," I said to myself in total shock and disgust. The host was supportive and quiet in his speech and reassured the gentleman that there might be a few things that would help him in this conference. Then the lady who meddled with my business blurted out to the guy, "I love you!"

"Please," I said to myself, "here's a guy here who needs a bona fide counselor and who is monopolizing the time that I have spent dollars to grow from, and the church lady is telling him she loves him! What's next, 'Kumbaya'?"

Then to make it worse, we were each asked by the host to tell this gentleman what attributes and qualities we saw in him that we appreciated. I thought I was going to lose it. There was nothing in that guy I wanted to affirm—except that he needed some serious help.

I listened as each one shared what he appreciated about this gentleman. I could just hear Robin Williams exclaiming, "Group hug!" I wasn't used to this syrupy stuff. And besides, what did group therapy have to do with leadership and presentation skills anyway? In my mind he just needed to "get over it."

Sadly, I came to realize how out of touch I truly was in that week-long event and how many relationships I had built with others who were equally out of touch.

I was blind and didn't think I was blind, but I was about to find out just how blind I had truly become. I don't believe I was "born" blind. I can remember a time when I was more open and receptive in my earlier years to what it really meant to "build" a sense of community. However, the drive to perform, succeed and "make things happen" got in the way of the greatness I was created to walk in.

My strong reaction was born out of my deep longing and frustration. Why is it such a crime to say "I love you" in the corporate world? Why is it so difficult to truly model it in areas of the church world? Isn't it strange that the One who said "judge not" has a multitude of followers who claim allegiance to Him while they disobey that edict, making carnally minded judgments regarding one another over and over again? Making value judgments of others' unmet needs deepens the rut of refined legalism that is killing the effectiveness of the church in society.

HIDING BEHIND A MASK

I wanted to "fix" this person at the seminar for his little "speck" that blocked his vision, while there was a glaring telephone pole sticking out of my own eye. It is dangerous to have head knowledge and not discern the need for the *experience* of truth.

The conference host spoke of the "masks" that Greek actors wore. We who have been in church for any length of time have heard this well-worn illustration. When Jesus and others use the word *hypocrite* in the New Testament, it is the Greek word for "wearing a mask." In other words, the face we show to others is not who we really are. Thus the audience never sees the real person; they hear the "voice of Jacob" behind the "mask of Esau," as it were. We have used the word in inflammatory tones to dehumanize someone who behaves in a way that we believe is incongruent.

I have come to believe, however, that in every admonition of Jesus and in every rebuke He gave to His disciples there was a spirit of longing and love that came through. We at times have turned the word *hypocrite* into the very thing that Jesus warned against. We exhibit "masking" behaviors and hide behind false facades in an effort to conceal our real identity. Usually it is because we are not sure how others are going to react to what they see behind the mask. We are afraid of the reaction of others because we are afraid of ourselves.

When the host began to talk about the word *hypocrite*, something in me wanted again to be the first one to answer his questions. After all, I was well versed in the Bible, and he obviously was wanting the "right answer." By that time something radically changed in my internal atmosphere. God was incredibly present to me in that room, and it was almost as though no one else was present except God and me. There have been several occasions when God would use an event as an epiphany, and light would dawn on an area of my darkness. This moment, however, was about to eclipse any others I had experienced subsequent to my conversion and the experience of the fullness of His Spirit.

JACK-IN-THE-BOX

The host reached behind his chair in the front of the room. Behind him was a large board leaning against the back of his chair. That large board concealed a number of props that he was going to use during his presentations throughout the week. He reached back behind the board and pulled out a very familiar childhood toy, the likes of which I hadn't seen since I was about five years old. I had seen others over the years that were more modernized, but this one was from the era in which I grew up.

One of my uncles worked for a season of his life for a toy import company in New York, and at Christmas he would give us the latest imports for presents. The host had no idea that I immediately recognized the make of the toy, because it was one of the lines that was imported by the New York company that my uncle used to work for. That alone released a flood of memories and emotions. In a moment of time I was reliving those moments when my uncle used to pull things out of a box for us at Christmas. Those were incredible moments for a little child. I had an "altar" in my memory to my childhood that this toy invited me to revisit.

Somehow I had a sense that what was about to take place was a set-up. The only problem was that no one in the room was behind the set-up, at least no one that I could see. The invisible hand of God began to direct the visible hand of the host as he stretched out his hand with the toy and placed it before me.

"Mark, do you know what this is?"

I said, "Of course! It is a jack-in-the-box!"

I wanted to proceed to tell him its vintage and the company that brought it into America. However, I knew it wasn't time to get into a history lesson about toys from the late 1950s.

The host asked me if I knew how it worked.

Now that is a dumb question, I thought to myself. I responded, "Why, of course!"

At that point the host asked me, "Would you mind demonstrating it for us?" Without giving me a chance to answer the question, he invited me to take the jack-in-the-box. I found my hand reaching out to take it while in my heart I was feeling quite silly and somewhat troubled.

I wasn't prepared for what happened next.

He asked me to describe how the toy worked before I demonstrated it. So I did. I actually knew a lot about the inner working of the jack-in-a-box. After I had (over) explained it, he then invited me to demonstrate its operation to the attendees.

The moment I put my hand on the crank my stomach was in knots. I didn't know where those feelings in my stomach were coming from, but they gripped me like a vise. As I turned the crank and the music played, inside of me I had a strong impression from God that sounded something like this: "This is Me, and I am doing something right now for your benefit. You really need this."

When we are in a tight place in the dark hallway of process, our minds can think faster than we have ever thought before, especially if we are looking for an escape hatch to flee the pain. Something was about to happen, *and I didn't want it to happen*. I needed to find a way out of the hallway quickly.

But once God catches you in the hallway, there is no escape. The only way out of the hallway is to go *through the hallway*. David said, "Yea, though I walk through..." the *hallway*.

When the tune completed its cycle, at the part where you would sing "pop goes the weasel," "jack" popped out of the box. He was dressed in a clown suit with a jester's hat, big white gloves and a blue-and-white polka-dot outfit—the height of fashion for a jack-in-the-box from the 1950s.

As the jack popped out of the box, something became unplugged inside my being, and out popped a flood of tears that was uncontrollable. Now I was both experiencing this and observing it at the same time. On the one hand I was sobbing for no apparent reason, and on the other hand I was embarrassed because I had lost my dignity in the presence of total strangers. Besides all that, *God let this happen*.

A legion of things was passing through me at that moment, none of which made any sense to the logical and suspicious side of my nature.

Within seconds the host said, "What's going on inside you, Mark?"

Again, it was as if no one was in the room. I wasn't even aware of who it was that was actually asking the question. My answer shocked my own ears.

For the first time in my life I admitted how I felt: "All my life I have been performing for others to get acceptance and approval. Whenever they 'turned the crank,' I would pop out of my little box and live up to their expectations. And when they were done with me, they would push me back down into those cramped quarters until they wanted me to perform again. *I am tired of popping out of the box and playing the clown!*"

The host said, "Wow!" (Pretty profound response, wouldn't you say?) He quietly waited while I tried to compose myself. Then he asked, *"Why have you chosen to stay in the box?"*

God was at it again, and I found myself confessing a litany of fears to total strangers. It was quite discomforting.

But then the strangest thing happened. Once I dumped all that stuff, I didn't give a rip about what anyone thought about me. *At a gut level, I felt a freedom I had not felt before.*

Then to keep me from taking myself too seriously, the "church lady" registrar piped up and said, "I knew God wanted you here, and I need you to know I love you!" I felt like Job when she made that statement. I said to myself, "The thing I feared greatly has come upon me!" (See Job 3:25.)

By the way, she was far from a "church lady." She was a greatly gifted and caring woman who loved God, and she was committed to drawing out the uniqueness of others in the best way that she knew, which was to offer them her affirming care and support. I later got to know her quite well and came to appreciate the depth of her years of wisdom. She actually taught the portion of the seminar on presentation skills and communication, and it was some of the most powerful training I have ever received on how to present a truth, expound it and then invite people to make a decision.

I could not have "heard" what she said in her sessions with all the masks I was wearing—I would have just added the information to my layers of performance and deepened my pain and frustration further.

After this dear lady said, "I love you," the troubled soul who had consumed half of our morning piped in and said, "Mark, I love you. You don't have to perform or pop out of a box for me to accept you!"

It would be hard to describe in words how the emotions now awakened inside of me were fighting to figure out who was in charge. I felt not so much like Dr. Jekyll and Mr. Hyde as much as I felt like Dr. McCoy and Spock in one of their many face-offs on *Star Trek*. There were two seemingly polar opposites in my makeup that were needing to be reconciled, and it was as if they met each other for the first time in the moment when "Jack" popped out of the box.

WATERSHED EXPERIENCES

This was a watershed for me, and from that point on illumination began to follow in my walk with God and my relationships with people. God used that silly toy to break through my defenses by first showing me myself and then healing my deep inner hurts.

By the power of His grace I was then able to make connections between my drive to get my unmet needs met and my inability to lead others into the future that God created them to experience. I was so preoccupied with my performance that I was never fully present to minister to the needs of others. I was present to my own need not to be rejected, not to be invisible and not to be abandoned. But as a result I couldn't be fully present to others.

My drive was based on my ego-driven pursuit of survival. Strangely enough, when you fail to discern the drive of your own unmet needs, you attract to yourself people with the same needs. Your relationships become driven by anything but intimacy and self-disclosure.

I didn't realize just how significant the jack-in-the-box incident was going to be to my future. It was obvious when I returned home that following weekend.

It was about midnight when I walked through the door to our home on Saturday night in North Carolina. My wife was awake and waiting up to welcome me home. I walked up the stairs to the second floor where our bedroom was. She was standing at the top of the stairs.

On the way up I looked into her eyes and said four little words: "Honey, I missed you!" When I got to the top of the stairs she gave me a hug, brought me near and whispered into my ear, "I don't know what has happened to you this week, but I want to marry you all over again!"

Now I was the one saying "Wow!" The seminar leader

used it, and now it was my turn. This was definitely a "wow" experience. Definitely.

Then it dawned on me: If I have been wearing masks all my life, then my voice was having to pass through the masks I was wearing. So then, while my voice was audible, it was still muffled behind the mask that I put in front of my face to hide the spot I didn't want anyone to see.

In essence, I realized that what my wife was saying without me having to tell her was that perhaps for the first time she heard the real me without any of the masks. She got more of me in four words than I was able to give her behind masks of performance for years. I was freer than I had ever been. Not only was I able to feel it, *but she felt it also.* Not only that, I didn't have to tell her or advertise that I had changed. It was evident— *the change spoke for itself.*

Incredible as it may seem, I had never been in such a place before. The chain reaction began immediately; my wife got a new husband, and my sons got a new father. The rest would follow in very short order. I had no idea as to what was awaiting me. I was about to trip over my treasure and didn't have a clue.

For whose attention and approval are you competing?

Destiny

is not

discovered—

it's

uncovered

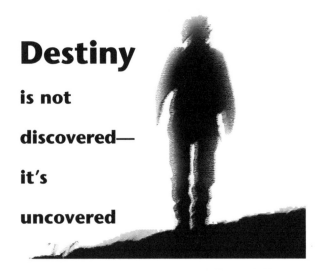

Tripping Over Treasure

Something wonderful, something hidden.
A gift unique to you. Find it.

—EMERSON

WHEN I WAS SEVEN YEARS OLD, MY COUSIN RONNIE AND I
went seeking buried treasure. Ronnie was a young artist.
Daily we pored over Marvel comic books while Ronnie
sketched our many comic book heroes. Together our
imaginations soared, along with our sense of adventure.

Having recently read *Treasure Island*, Ronnie and I
decided to search for hidden treasure. We scavenged
through our grandmother's garage on Bement Avenue
for hoes, shovels and other tools. Armed, we began
digging up Grandma's back yard. It wasn't long before

we discovered our treasure. We unearthed a handful of metal medallions that had been used to announce a circus. We were thrilled. We carefully placed our treasure in a shoebox and guarded our wonderful discovery for a very long time.

Something deep within us calls to seek hidden treasure. As I've read the parable of the hidden treasure in Matthew 13:44, a question jumps off the page. The man was wandering, and he found himself in a field with treasure. Then he happened to trip over it and uncovered it. But what was in him that caused him to seek that treasure?

He had a homing device deep within him. It was serendipitous. He couldn't give a *why* or a *wherefore*, but something in him told him, "I've got to dig." So he began to dig, and he uncovered something that he was meant to find. Buried under all that dirt in the field was a call that called him forth.

This treasure hunter didn't realize that what was in him was also in the box of treasure. It was a deep calling unto deep that went beyond words.

I returned home from the week-long event so refreshed that I was ready to dive right into my world and get busy. The difference, however, posed a challenge for me. I had lived my life up until that point as a "jack-in-the-box." But now I was out of the box—and I wasn't going back. God had invited me to discover a more inspired viewing point. He had provided a way for me to escape the confines of "the box," and He was inviting me to go to a higher place. From there I would gain a more inspired view of the things He had prepared for me to walk in.

I knew I was walking away from everything I had done prior to that moment. I was in a season of redefining. My crisis catapulted me out of the world I had known into the hallway of the unknown. Now I was being invited to experience what I had never known. This was my invitation to step into greatness.

My teaching style began to change—and so did my message content. I was no longer merely interested in giving out a lot of information. I no longer wanted to speak about a depth of revelation that was not congruent with my level of experience. Many times our intellects can grasp truths that are way beyond our level of experience, but that does not bring lasting change or transformation to our lives or to the lives of those whom we are leading.

UNCOVERING DESTINY

Waking up to a larger life was only the beginning. My core values were clearer because I wasn't hiding from myself anymore. I had built the walls of my dream on ground that was not capable of holding the weight of divine destiny. Once I had built the walls and was climbing the ladder to put the roof of success on my plans, I discovered that the ladder was leaning on a wall that was about to fall. Falling from that height would have been excruciating. But in the mercy of God I was made aware that my ladder was leaning on the wrong wall when "jack" popped out of the box.

As I walked away from the way I had done things previously, without knowing it I was walking toward a new way of being the person God called me to be. Destiny isn't something we *discover*—it's something we *uncover*.

There comes a moment in our lives when we find that certain things no longer have the appeal they used to have. The drive to have more and do more loses its grip. Hallway travel can slow you down quite a bit. Then the drive to be better, based as it is on comparison and competition, loses its appeal. Why do we need to be better than someone else?

At that strategic moment in the hallway when "jack" popped out of the box, I realized that I had spent a great deal of time trying to be better than others just to get the approval of my father. Why couldn't I just be the best me that God wanted me to be? The drive to be different loses its appeal when that becomes sufficient.

There can be a drive in us to be different just so that someone will see us as unique individuals. *The harder you try to prove that you are different, the more you actually prove that you are just like everybody else who is leaning their ladder on the wrong wall.*

I was walking away from the tree where I had fed on the need to have more and do more, have what was better and do what was better, have what was different and be what was different.

Turning in the direction of the tree of life, I heard something deep within me, something deeper than my hidden spot and deeper than my blind spot. There was a treasure hidden in the recesses of my heart calling my name. It had the resonance of God when it called, and its sound was pure, peaceable, gentle, reasonable, full of mercy and good fruits, unwavering and without hypocrisy.

Looking for Something—
and Finding Something Far Greater

I felt like the merchant who walked away from everything he had built in the city and was kicking around in
a field far from town when he stumbled and tripped
over something that got his attention. (See Matthew
13:44.) He didn't know what he was looking for. *But he
did know he was looking for something—and the
"something" that he found was a treasure.* Something
deep within was searching. But he found this treasure
quite by accident when his feet tripped over what he
was not looking for.

The Greek word for "found" actually means that he
found it without previous search, that he found it by
chance—that he fell in with it. What was this?
Serendipity of the highest order. We trip over a treasure
we don't know has our name on it! That is what the
kingdom of God within us is all about.

According to the parable, the man bought the field
from the owner. But first he buried the treasure from
view so that no one would steal it. He then made a
return trip to his former manner of life where he had
"made a living" instead of building a life, and he "sold
all that he had" in order to buy the field.

That was the only way to get the treasure—they went
together. The field was probably nothing to look at—a
parched parcel of land covered with rocks and boulders,
as so much of the land is in that part of the world.

The more he thought about it, the more wisdom he
saw in the serendipity that the treasure was hidden in
the least likely place. Once he bought the field, he was

able to take possession of the treasure. If the treasure was more valuable than anything he had ever had in his life before, then nothing he had "built" could adequately house the treasure he had just acquired. The field then became the place where there was space to build something that was an adequate reflection of the worth of the treasure. The merchant rebuilt his life in a new place, encompassing an existing, yet uncovered, treasure, formerly hidden in darkness and now brought into full view.

When he "tripped" over the treasure, it dawned on him that while he didn't know where to find what he was looking for in all the old familiar places, there in that isolated remote field he tripped over what he had been searching for all his life. The kingdom of heaven is like a treasure hidden in a field. And as we step into greatness, we will uncover the greatest treasure we have ever seen—our unique, God-given destiny.

What are you chasing that you are not supposed to find?

Find the

courage to

ask for your

missing piece

Asking for the
Missing Piece

Most of us are so busy doing what we
have to do, that we do not think about
what we really want to do.
—ROBERT PERCIVAL

GETTING TO THE CORE OF A MATTER AND THE HEART
of an issue is not always easy. There is a core upon
which a real and genuine life can be built, shaped and
formed for greatness. But more often than not it is
buried under layers of disappointment, frustration,
unfinished business, judgments, fears and anxieties.

The Disney animated feature *Peter Pan* was released

when I was about five years old. Uncle Danny, my dad's youngest brother, took all my cousins and me to see it one night at the St. George Theater. As I recall, it was one of my first visits to the theater.

The theater had a big stage with a large billowing, red velvet curtain. There were ornate sculptured faces and figures in gold leafing on the sides of the stage rising to the top of the ceiling. I remember the orchestra pit and the big theater organ sitting right in the middle. The balcony was as big as the first floor, and at five years old it was the most incredible building I had ever been in. The screen was so much bigger than our Du Pont television set at home. It went wall to wall and floor to ceiling. When the movie started, I was on the edge of my seat, and I stayed there throughout. I remember being so excited when I saw the ship flying in the air. I believed in a dream for the future from that moment on.

When we left the theater, my cousins Bobby and Ronnie and I began to talk about what we wanted to do with our lives. Pretty deep stuff for two five-year-olds and a seven-year-old. Since Bobby was older, that meant he was wiser. On the way back from the movies, we sat together in the back seat of Uncle Danny's red Plymouth Lancer and whispered about some secret plans we were making. We wanted to go to Disneyland and experience the "Pirates of the Caribbean" and all of the other fun stuff that we saw on "The Wonderful World of Color." The movie just heightened our longings.

When we arrived at Grandma's house where our parents were, Bobby, Ronnie and I escaped to a quiet place to discuss our secret plan. You see, Bobby planned to build an airplane, and only we were to know about it.

This was top secret information. In Bobby's garage was an old baby carriage that was still in great shape. He said there was also an old gas lawn mower blade sitting there, a few big wooden crates, an old steering wheel and a pedal car they didn't ride anymore.

Bobby and Ronnie planned to get the wheels and chassis from the carriage and place big wooden crates on top, fastening them to the wheels. They would then take pedals from the pedal car and connect them to the bottom. Then they planned to hook up the lawn mower blade to the front to make a propeller. Afterward they would hook up an old steering wheel to the front of the first crate and rig it to the "propeller" to steer the thing.

The next morning, before anybody knew it, Bobby and Ronnie were going to fly this contraption from Elm Street to Bement Avenue and swoop down and pick me up from my bedroom window on the second floor at Grandma's house. The estimated time of arrival was about 6 A.M., which was just before our dads went to work. Bobby said we would be in Disneyland within a few short hours.

I was so excited.

I believed everything Bobby said to me, and why not? He was the smartest in his class, could do math in his head, was a great speller—and he was *two years older* than Ronnie and me.

That night I went into my closet and grabbed my stickball bat and laid it on my bed. Grandpa used to use these big red and white neckerchiefs when he was loading and unloading coal, and he had given me a brand-new one that was in my dresser drawer. I didn't know what a neckerchief was, except that Grandpa tied it around his neck and sweat a lot in it when he was working. It was a whole lot bigger than a handkerchief and too pretty to blow your nose in.

I sneaked into the kitchen while Mom and Dad were in the living room, opened the refrigerator and pulled out a package of Arnold Dinner Rolls. I then grabbed a jar of Skippy Peanut Butter from the closet. I brought the rolls and peanut butter back into the bedroom.

As I recall, I grabbed a pair of socks and an extra undershirt and shorts and folded them all neatly in the red and white neckerchief. Then I tied the neckerchief to the stickball bat the way I had seen Spanky do it on *The Little Rascals* when he ran away from home. I put my "travel kit" by the bedroom window, and when it was time to go to sleep, I decided to keep the shade of my window open that night. I could hardly sleep—I was on my way to Disneyland!

I was wide-awake at 5 A.M. when Dad got up to get ready for work. I waited until he was in the bathroom before I hopped out of bed and got dressed. He usually took a long time to get ready for work, so I figured I would be gone by the time he got out of the bathroom.

I had my "travel kit" in my hand, and I stood at that second-floor window waiting. At any moment, Bobby and Ronnie were going to come flying to the second floor—just like the ship in *Peter Pan*—and pick me up so we could go to Disneyland.

By the time Dad was done in the bathroom, I was still waiting for my flight to arrive. I was tempted to call Bobby on the phone. However, I didn't want to give our secret away. I just kept waiting and expecting.

Dad noticed me standing at the window and asked me

why I wasn't in bed. I did my best not to tell him the secret, and he did his best to encourage me to go back to bed.

I guess you figured out by now that Bobby's idea never got off the ground—in spite of his considerable seven-year-old ingenuity. However, the impression that idea left in me has remained with me for quite a long time. Later that afternoon when Bobby and Ronnie came over to Grandma's house, he explained some of the construction problems that he faced—but not to worry, he was still working on it.

Twenty-eight years later I got off a plane in Southern California and headed in a taxi to a hotel in Anaheim.

I had never been in California before, and I didn't know where Anaheim was in relation to anything. I was scheduled to speak at a conference that was beginning the next day. Thousands were registered, and it was a four-day event. I was a day early and had two days following the conference to relax. My wife and I decided to make the most of our time while we were there.

On the way to the hotel we passed by the entrance to Disneyland. Since I had never been to California before, I had no clue that Disneyland was in the neighborhood. When I got there and walked through the entrance, I found myself reconnecting with the memory of that moment at the second-floor window of my bedroom. I found myself saying in my heart, "Bobby, I really made it to Disneyland—*and I even got to fly!*"

DREAMS AND DESIRES

Some dreams take longer to realize than others, and

they don't always get fulfilled quite the way we expect. In that great hymn "Praise to the Lord, the Almighty," the hymn writer penned these words:

> Hast thou not seen
> How thy desires e'er have been
> Granted in what *He ordaineth*! [1]

God places desires within the core of our being. Written on the tablets of our hearts is the destiny of God. Some embrace it, while others never even wake up to it.

I believe in the power of dreams and in the nature of desire. Both are God's idea. God is the greatest Dreamer of all. At times it may seem as though life is arrayed against the dream of your life. It's all part of the process.

THE KINGDOM OF HEAVEN

The kingdom of heaven is as expansive as heaven. God called *the expanse* "heaven." It is the nature of heaven to grow and expand. The kingdom has many dimensions to its scope and influence.

One of those dimensions is this: It is *within us*. There is uniqueness to the expression of God's kingdom in our life. Christ in you is uniquely different in expression than Christ in *me*. We are all one-of-a-kind, never-to-be-repeated masterpieces. There is a "dream of destiny" relative to the grand purpose of God that finds its expression in our life *in a way that can be revealed through no other*. We were not made to be "clones" of someone else.

I want to remind you of Walter Brueggemann's statement that "idolatry is second-hand living." The belief that you should have been born someone else, in some other time, in some other place or under some other circumstances is to fail to grasp that the Master Potter created you with specific outcomes in mind. You—as you—bring an expression of God's creativity to life in a way that no one else ever could or would be able to, because they are not you.

I "tripped" over my treasure when I walked away from the manner in which I had previously conducted my life. My "jack-in-the-box" days were over—I had popped out of the box for the last time. I wasn't ever going to go back in there again. I wanted the "wide-open spaces." David said, "Thou hast set my feet in a large place" (Ps. 31:8). Eugene Peterson paraphrases David's words this way: "You...gave me room to breathe" (THE MESSAGE). I was just beginning to get in touch with the spaciousness of a larger life in God.

The word *desire* comes from the Latin language, and when we take it through its etymology and distill it down to what it means, it boils down to "something is missing." In other words, desire has to do with a *missing piece* in the puzzle of life. Jesus said, "Whatever you *desire*..." Imagine that! Whatever is our missing piece, when we pray, believe that we already have been given it, and we shall have it. Consider the missing piece in this fashion: "Whatever is from your Father that you have not yet fully realized or experienced and that you long for and know is missing..."

Who owns "the field of dreams" where our treasure is waiting to be tripped over? Whose treasure is it anyway? Looked at one way, the treasure in the field is the earth itself, and the merchant is the Son of God.

But in light of the Savior's words that the kingdom of heaven is within us, there is another way to look at the parable. The field is the undeveloped and unaffirmed areas of our life where God has hidden the greatest treasure of all. He hid it where we would be least likely to look: deep in the unknown spot of our hearts from where dreams come. There the treasure is awaiting the moment when we are ready to leave the familiar and launch out into a life of adventure, where we are led by God in the dance of destiny. The journey toward greatness begins with a single awkward step. But even if we trip at first, soon we find ourselves being led into the thing we have been missing all our life.

To miss something, or desire something, implies by those very longings that we believe that the missing things exist *somewhere*. *Where they are* is as elusive at times as *what they are*. Nevertheless, it is the question of "where is my missing piece" that leads us on the quest to find it.

As I emerged out of the hallway of God's refining process, I began to learn how to pace myself in every relationship, to let go of my tendencies to "mask" and to become genuinely transparent. My prayers took on a deeper and more intimate tone. I felt what David spoke of as the "nearness of God" when he said, "But as for me, it is good to be near God. I have made the Sovereign LORD my refuge" (Ps. 73:28, NIV).

I began experiencing insight into my life and my patterns of behavior. I was letting go of value judgments and the bitter roots in my personal history that were blocking my view of intended destiny. I was better able to recognize where I had been "hooked" by the lie and caught in the snare of the fowler. My desires were being freed from my expectations. In that, I discovered that my performance-oriented, masking lifestyle had caused me to experience the reality of my expectations, which included being disappointed, being let down and a whole host of other things tied to my unmet needs.

Now that I was letting go of those expectations, my desires were allowed to surface and lead me in a direction I never thought I would go. I began to press into relationships with a different posture. I was learning how to be fully present to others because the internal noise of my formerly unfinished business was growing quiet.

Certainly there are still areas in me that catch me off guard from time to time. But today the "joys" of living in the moment and being present to God, present to others and present to myself are progressively crowding out the patterns of my yesterdays.

I had "sold everything I had," and I had enough from the exchange to buy the field of dreams and the treasure that was buried in it.

I was about to be redefined. I was about to pass through the end of the hallway and step into greatness.

What is your heart searching for that refuses to be denied?

The

**substance of
things hoped
for, the title
deed of things
not seen**

14

Stepping Into Greatness

> When one door closes, another door
> opens; but we often look so longingly
> and so regretfully upon the door that
> closed that we fail to see the one that
> has opened for us.
>
> —HELEN KELLER

ROBERT K. GREENLEAF, THE LEGENDARY AUTHORITY
on management and leadership, once gave an address
that was entitled, *Have You a Dream Deferred?* These
are his remarkable words:

I hope you will manage your lives...so that you

leave the university with a well-set style of greatness, with attitudes and values and ways of initiating and responding that will assure service in the public interest with distinction. Distinction is not synonymous with fame. Whether your life is long or short or your opportunities large or small, *distinction or greatness* is a combination of the moral and the excellent. It is doing the very best you can with the talents you have and the opportunities you can find.

Your vocation can be any legitimate calling your talents justify, be you poet, scientist or businessman. A lifestyle of greatness will augur for total impact that will leave some segment of society a little better than if you had not tried. It is important that some of you make this choice now because plenty of people, by design or accident, will leave it worse. It takes a lot of hard work by responsible individuals for a society just to stay even. (*I use the word "responsible" advisedly.* I am not using it in the same sense that so many of my generation use it when what they mean is that they want you to behave so that their comfort, their sense of propriety, are not disturbed. Responsible people build; they do not destroy. They are moved by the heart. The prime test of rightness of an act is: How will it affect people, are lives moved toward nobility?)[1]

Prior to my experience in the hallway I spent much time committed to making things happen. I was going to hang in there no matter what, just to see something through to completion. God, however, wanted me to step into a place where I let things happen of their own accord. Life in God is going somewhere according to a much grander design than I could ever ask, think or even imagine. I can sing "I Surrender All" and still hold on tightly and not let go.

JABBOK

Jacob's pilgrimage brought him to the ford of the river Jabbok (the place of emptying), where all of his excess baggage was finally "dumped" in the fork in the river. The baggage went in one direction, and he went in another. He had finally lost all the extra weight.

What he hadn't lost was his tenacity and his determination. As day was about to break, the fear-driven and yet powerful Jacob, who thought he had been wrestling all night with his brother Esau, discovered that, when the light began to dawn and his blindness was being healed, he was wrestling with another Man.

God is the only one who can handle your unfinished business, process you through all its pain, let you wrestle with Him and make you feel like a winner (almost)! When dawn broke over the Jabbok River, Jacob felt like a winner for the first time in his life. Someone finally let him experience winning. One thing remained, however. Jacob wanted a guarantee that his life would be different from that moment on. He wanted the blessing—not the fake one, the real one! He said, "I won't let You go until You bless me!"

In the hallway, even though I had been through the process, I still was hanging on tightly to the cords of what I thought was my purpose. I held on because I was afraid of missing God's best. I was committed to fulfilling my destiny. I was holding on tightly so I could be blessed. That is how I learned to survive. Hold on tight and hang in there—no matter what—until you accomplish whatever it was you were supposed to accomplish.

BLESSING COMES BY LETTING GO

It is amazing how often the story of Jacob at the river has been taught incorrectly. We have encouraged people to hang on to God until the blessing comes because of this story, when God basically said, "Blessing doesn't come by hanging on—it comes by letting go."

The Lord said, "Let Me go." When Jacob refused, God touched the "hollow place" where he leaned all his weight for balance in his walk. The walk of faith is not balanced until God touches the hollow place where we have tried to lean on our own efforts. Once He has touched us, He then invites us to limp into the future—but only after we realize that the way to hold on tightly is to let go. Holding the reins of destiny loosely is the only way to surrender to God and experience the greatness of His destiny for us. We are participants in something much larger than ourselves. Surrendering to the "flow" of that at the ford of the Jabbok is where we are emptied of all the patterns of holding on so that we move in a totally different direction.

The blessing Jacob needed wasn't more money, livestock or family (he had quite a large family by now). He needed to know it was OK for him to be whom he was born to be. *Yet whom was he born to be?* He had never been affirmed for who he truly was.

A New Name for a New Day

From birth his parents labeled him "heel grabber" after his first "performance." That label and name shaped his life. It became a self-fulfilling prophecy.

In order to step into greatness, he needed to have his identity affirmed by the one true Significant Other. The Lord of hosts was well able to *evoke* from him what He had *invoked* within him.

So the Lord asked him a question: "What is your name?"

The now limping one replied, "Heel Catcher."

The Lord's reply was essentially this: "Now that you have admitted to yourself and to Me who you have been, I am going to rename you based on who you are about to become! Your new name is 'Prevailing Prince of Power with God and Man!'" (See Genesis 32:28.)

Wow! Jacob had just found out who he had been and who he was becoming. He had been his own worst enemy. He had been on the lam his whole life—not from Esau—*but from himself*. Esau was never his real problem.

When Jacob was affirmed for who he truly was, he recognized who the Man was with whom he had been wrestling. He asked Him His name—and didn't get a reply. The One who names us cannot be named by us, for that would make us the controllers of that which is beyond us. We are named for His purpose—He is not named for ours. So the Man said, "Why is it that you ask My name?" Israel had now come to see God in some concrete and human context. Once his blind spot is recognized and his hidden spot is disclosed, his unknown spot begins to rise, and in a moment of truth he who once was blind now can see all things clearly. He named the place "Peniel," which means "the face of God."

At that moment, the Man departed from view, and Israel "limped" over that ground where a loser became a winner. A man hiding under his brother's skins found safety, acceptance and his true identity.

FROM BLAMING TO BLESSING

Esau was still on the way, and they were now walking toward each other. Israel couldn't run from his past since he had reconciled it to himself in the presence of God. Jacob had spent his days running from his past, but Israel was now limping into his future. He was pacing himself a bit more slowly and enjoying the scenery. He wasn't even afraid any longer of what his brother might try to do to him. As a matter of fact, he was no longer angry with Esau—he no longer had any need to blame his brother for his pain.

Once he *saw* himself for who he was in the presence of the other Man and *accepted* himself without having to hide, *he could accept Esau for who he was*. There was not a word of anger or hatred shared, only an embrace and tears of joy. Israel wanted to "give" his brother what he never could give him before from a heart of love and acceptance.

What Israel didn't know was that while he was working through his unfinished business with God, Esau had also been working through his unfinished business with God. They were reconciled to each other in a moment of embrace, and the Invisible Man was responsible for it all. Israel said these powerful words to his brother, "I see your face as one sees the face of God" (Gen. 33:10). Jesus said, "Blessed are the pure [undivided, singular vision and focus] in heart, for they shall see God" (Matt. 5:8). Who better to know what God's face looks like than the one who just wrestled with Him all night long and finally recognized Him for who He is?

Israel was now able to see the "image of God" and the greatness of God in the brother from whom he was formerly estranged. When we see ourselves for whom we truly are meant to be in God, we can begin to call others out of their limited ways of seeing into the limitless reality of seeing all things as having been wrought in God.

Wow!

I was opening up in ways I had never opened up before and was obtaining outcomes I had never experienced before (however, that is for another book). Within a matter of weeks I was making incredible connections with people I had always wanted to meet but never expected to get to know. People were just "showing up" in planes, hotels, conferences—you name it.

I wasn't "working the floor"; I was just enjoying being alive. I started getting phone calls from leaders who wanted to have me speak to their networks of leaders. Wow again! Never in my wildest imagination could I have dreamed that up. This was new, and I couldn't figure it out.

I was crying a whole lot more, but not because of unfinished business. *I was crying for joy* and really giving myself permission to have all my feelings without masking them. I was learning how to describe them rather than have them describe me in a moment of crisis.

THE INVITATION

A few weeks later I was in bed and sound asleep. At 3 A.M. sharp I was awakened. The red digital letters on the alarm clock of my night table brought back the grim remembrance of the six months of night visits that I had endured. I didn't know what to expect when I turned over and looked at the foot of the bed.

There at the foot of the bed was a bright and very warm light in the "shape" of a cloud. It was dark everywhere in the room, except where the light was at the foot of the bed. I wasn't sure what was happening, but I was feeling a deep sense of peace and warmth.

I got out of bed as the light began to move toward the doorway and out of the bedroom. I walked toward the doorway and went to turn on the lights. Something inside me knew that I had to go downstairs into the living room. As I approached the bottom of the first landing between the first story and the second story, I went to reach for the light so that I could negotiate my way down the rest of the stairs to the living room. But as I went to reach for the light, I knew intuitively that I was not to turn it on. So I proceeded to walk down the rest of the stairs in the dark.

We lived in a house that had a lot of windows on the main floor with a large two-story deck off the kitchen. It has a Florida room off the back of the house, and the glass afforded lots of light on the main floor. Every night before retiring, Ruth and I would have to close every set of blinds on the windows in the house. The main floor was quite a chore. For some reason we had closed every set of blinds except the largest blind on the largest window facing the back of the house. We lived on a golf course that overlooked the ninth hole. The view was gorgeous.

The blinds were open, and the moonlight was coming through. The pattern of the blinds and the rays created a shaft of light in the middle of the living room floor that actually formed a circle. Against the backdrop of the dark room, it was absolutely beautiful.

I had only experienced a few encounters with the angelic that I could remember, but I was aware that I had followed a heavenly messenger to the spot where I was standing. It was an awesome moment, and I didn't know what to expect. I felt drawn toward the circle of moonlight on the floor, and as I approached, the angel left.

I had just completed a teaching on the sun, moon and stars and their symbolic significance in the Scriptures. The moon illumines by reflected light. As such, it is a "witness" to the light of the sun, even though the sun is not visible at night. So then the moon is a symbol for faith in the midst of adversity.

I have already mentioned my personal "hallway of process" and how dark it had been. The moonlight became a living metaphor for my own faith that had guided me during the night season I had gone through. Faith is a witness to the light of God's glory when we are in the dark hallway between a former day and a new day.

I was becoming persuaded, after all those years of walking in less than God's best, that He was still faithful, for the sake of the future, to keep that which I had committed to Him. (See 2 Timothy 1:12.)

I began to see the beauty of this shaft of light that was just one step in front of me, and I wondered what awaited me in the days ahead.

Just then I heard a voice, not audible, within my spirit. It commanded, "Step into greatness!"

I wanted to argue with that voice because I felt I didn't know what "greatness" was. I knew it wasn't fame, fortune or anything like that. I wasn't as confident as I had been in my ability to define things, and I was uncomfortable trying to step into something I could not quite define.

Nevertheless, the voice persisted in my spirit and again commanded, "Step into greatness." I began to feel silly. After all, here I am standing in the middle of my living room at 3 A.M. arguing with God over whether or not this was really happening and wondering what the big deal was about light from the moon on the living room floor.

At that moment, I was reminded of all the seemingly

foolish prophetic acts throughout the flow of history that changed and shaped the future. Taking arrows and striking the ground in the bedchamber of a prophet seemed a silly way to win a battle against invading armies. Sending out musicians to face a marauding band of murderers seemed a pretty low-yield solution to gain a victory over a determined and ruthless foe.

It didn't matter where I was in the house. It didn't matter if anyone saw me in the secret place doing something "foolish." It did matter that I present my heavenly Father with a willing spirit.

The third time I heard the invitation, I let go of my "rational sense of judgment," and I stepped into the reflected light of the moon cast on the carpet of my living room floor.

As I did, all at once something deep within me opened up. I had stepped into the awesome presence of a holy God. Surrounded in glory, I began to weep. This time, however, I wasn't weeping from the place of pain. I wept from a deep, unknown place within me where the "treasure" of the kingdom had been buried, awaiting this moment of its uncovering. I was weeping for the future for which God had created me. I was longing for that which He created me to do.

There in that moment, I felt the assurance that He was going to do things for me that I could never do for myself. He was about to bring me to a place of serving Him that I never could have orchestrated.

As I stood there bathed in that light, I heard one final question: "Ask Me for a sign!" I had never been told by God to ask for a sign. This was beyond me.

A certain notable minister, whom I deeply admired,

was planning a large event in a major metropolitan area in a few months. Such events require time and extensive coordination. Speakers are booked well in advance of the actual event. But this event was less than three months away and was being advertised nationally. So this was the sign: I asked to speak at that event. This was important to me because now I believed I truly had something to say that could help others navigate their way through their own unfinished business.

I lingered for a few more moments in prayer, and then I quietly and peacefully went back upstairs and fell asleep.

As I was journaling at my computer the next day, I wrote these words: In the pursuit of your life's purpose, there will strategically occur a defining moment in the form of a refining crisis setting you free from a confining limitation, thus empowering you to *step into greatness!*

I began to frame a whole series of teachings on the insights I learned and the transition I experienced. I was moving forward and seeing outcomes I never thought possible.

CONFIRMATION

About a month after my encounter with my heavenly messenger, I was at a large conference where we were doing a workshop. Our product display needed to be set up in the vendor's area, and we needed an outside line for credit card orders. It took about forty-five minutes to get an outside line to our booth. Once we did, the hotel brought us an extra long phone cord to plug into a far wall and then connect to the phone at our tape and book booth. As I was plugging in the jack at the far wall, my assistant was plugging in the jack to the phone.

I walked away to take care of some other errands. When I returned to the booth, my assistant was hanging up the phone. She said that such and such a person had called on behalf of "so and so."

"Really?" I asked. "What did they want?"

"They were calling to see if you are available to speak at their next major event as a main speaker."

"Why did they call me?"

"They felt impressed after prayer that you were to be one of the speakers at the event."

It was *exactly* the sign I had asked for—something so out of the ordinary that only God could do it.

The rest is history and destiny—not just mine, but yours as well. There are serendipitous events awaiting you in the unfolding order of God's incredible purpose for your life.

There is unfinished business to complete, unknown paths to walk in and unknown treasure to uncover.

Make the decision to move into the future. Godspeed to you as you *step into greatness*!

What would you have the courage to ask for if you knew the answer was yes?

Notes

1. Consider these words of biblical scholar Meredith Kline in his landmark work, *Kingdom Prologue, Volume I:* "The key phrase describing God's approach through the garden, traditionally translated 'in the cool of the day,' should be rendered 'as the Spirit of the day.' *Spirit* here denotes the theophanic Glory, as it does in Genesis 1:2 and elsewhere in Scripture. And 'the day' has the connotation it often has in the prophet's forecasts of the great coming judgment. Here in Genesis 3:8 is the original day of the Lord, which served as a prototypal mold in which subsequent pictures of other days of the Lord were cast. Such a day is one of divine epiphany. The final such day is the day of our Lord's *Parousia*, the day of His presence as the personal revelation of the glory with the clouds and the angels of heaven. Significantly, *panim*, meaning 'face or presence,' one of the biblical designations of the Glory-Spirit, is referred to in Genesis 3:8, and accordingly what is depicted there is nothing less than the primal *Parousia*. On the original day of the Lord in Eden, God's *parousia*-advent was in the theophanic mode of 'the Spirit (Presence) of the day (of judgment).' Trumpeting the advent of the Divine Presence—at Sinai, at Pentecost, at the *Parousia* of Jesus, at every

day of the Lord—is the fearful sound of the voice of the Lord, the thunderclap of the approaching theo-phanic storm-chariot. It was by precisely this arresting signal that the primal *Parousia* was her-alded. Alarmed by this sound of God's coming, the man and his wife sought escape, of all places, in the area of the judgment tree."

2. Thomas A. Kane, *Happy Are You Who Affirm* (n.p.: House of Affirmation, 1976).

3. Leanne Payne, *The Healing Presence* (Wheaton, IL: Crossway Books, 1989), 47–48. "Practicing His Presence, we live decisively out of that new self. To practice His Presence, therefore, is also to practice the presence of the new man (self) rather than the old. The soul, with its new center in Christ radically changed and redirected, is to be accepted. There is the oddest thing about the history of Christian teaching. This new, real self is largely ignored, feared or even denied. If one doubts this, he need simply run through the references in the best Bible helps. There the old or false self is catalogued and refer-enced in every possible way, which is absolutely good and necessary. But where is the real self acknowl-edged? It goes largely uncelebrated, unreferenced, and in effect unaccepted. For the 'walk in the Spirit,' the true self is required. Is this why we are so back-ward in teaching what the 'walk in the Spirit' really is? It is no wonder that Christians have a hard time with *self-acceptance, a moral as well as Christian virtue necessary to Christian living in Christ.*

"Until this redeemed self is acknowledged and accepted, we live out of the immature, unaffirmed self, and we cannot hear God aright. From that center we also 'mishear' our fellows, and they become the target of the diseased 'matter' that yet resides within our souls—that is, our fears of rejection, our bitterness, envy, anger, and sense of inferiority. These invariably project themselves into the minds and hearts of those we love the most, piercing them like deadly arrows. Until we *accept the new self,* we are dangerous to ourselves and to others; even though we are Christians, we are still enthralled by the voices of this world and obey them. We fail to abide in Christ and instead remain self-conscious."

CHAPTER 9
BECOMING WHO YOU ARE

1. Walter Brueggeman, *Living Toward a Vision: Biblical Reflections on Shalom* (Cleveland, OH: United Church Press, 1976).

CHAPTER 10
DIPPING INTO DESTINY

1. J. Wallace Hamilton, *Serendipity* (Old Tappan, NJ: Fleming H. Revell Company, 1965).

CHAPTER 11
UNCOVERING YOUR UNIQUENESS

1. David C. Needham, *Birthright: Christian, Do You Know Who You Are?* (Sisters, OR: Multnomah Press, 1979).

CHAPTER 13
ASKING FOR THE MISSING PIECE?

1. "Praise to the Lord, the Almighty" by Joachim Neander (translated by Catherine Winkworth), public domain.

CHAPTER 14
STEPPING INTO GREATNESS

1. Robert K. Greenleaf, *The Power of Servant Leadership* (San Francisco: Berrett-Koehler Publishers, 1998).

Dr. Chironna has other books, audio and video product available. To obtain a product or catalog or to request more information about Dr. Chironna's ministry, please write:

Mark Chironna Ministries
7512 Dr. Phillips Blvd.
Suite 50-360
Orlando, FL 32819

Or you may call (407) 826-4777 or visit his website at www.markchironna.com.